7 Principles Of Highly Effective Tech People

Anna Kristina Paulson

Since I started my career eight years ago, I worked for an average size IT consulting company from Germany and undertook the challenges posed by Information Technology. Settling into the role of a Front-end and Database Developer, I had to deal with more than just technical complications as various issues came my way, especially relating to communicating efficiently between teams and maintaining healthy work-life balance.

A significant challenge was understanding the subtle nuances of communication between IT professionals and their non-technical colleagues. A bridge was needed to unite these two unique worlds, a task which could only be carried out respectively by the human translator such as a reader of Chinese scrolls intricately scripted in the language of geek-speak. At the same time, a fine balance between work and family life has taken the shape of a major issue exposed lurking in dark shadows running across the professional arena.

At the end of my career in the IT field, I changed careers and became a coach and a psychologist. This transition allowed me to incorporate the insights earned from an evaluation of the IT environment with psychological perceptions. These experiences merged to generate a singular perspective, and provided an integrated view of the issues faced by industries in the field of technology.

Working with the themes that have surprised and intrigued me, this book is a reflective narrative about my experiential insights, an alternative to the dominant coding-oriented discourse. As such, rather than trying to encompass a wider narrative; it looks at the complex relationships found within IT environments. Through the following chapters, we go on a pragmatic quest for challenges, solutions and principles to ensure routine professional relationship is more consensual and productive.

We are exploring how the involved parties communicate, and our process further unravels the modalities of communication between IT and non-IT bodies. The text goes even further to narrate a highly complex, never-ending interaction of striking that perfect work life balance issue which professional veterans often miss the mark. What a reader finds behind each principle presented is not just an abstract construct but its character stems from concrete scenes that emerged by engaging in the IT environment.

The success of the paradigm of the seven principles lies in its pragmatism and inclusiveness, addressing a wide range of issues faced by technophiles. It is taken up in its wide acceptance because it connects to understand the present-day emerging situation in the modern tech landscape.

To begin with, the popularity of paradigm is attributed to its simplicity and ease in understanding. It directs away from unnecessary oversimplification to support technical language, making it all encompassing and reader friendly. This simplicity makes people to realize what has happened and hence easy understanding and implementation independently of their technical capabilities.

Moreover, the progressing popularity of the paradigm is partly related to its flexibility. It does not dish out stale, one size fits all unviable solutions. It rather offers a dynamic framework that is tailored in such a way to be adaptable for different settings within the context of the tech. This flexibility is critically important in a role of an information environment that has never been, and probably will be never the same again by virtue of rapid changes in technology employed, methodologies used together to arrive at project requirements.

The incorporation of soft skills into the paradigm is another reason accounting for its international boom. The paradigm is also based on the recognition of collaboration, communication, and problem-solving beside technical ability as well important parts of work performance that match with our third premise accepting this holistic set skill demanded at modern jobs. The practice of inclusivity embraced by this framework deeply speaks to professionals who desire success in group and interdisciplinary environments.

In addition, this paradigm has the agile methodologies subscribed to it to make it easy for the implementation of such a paradigm. With the adoption of agile practices in project management, this new paradigm emerges as the trend and reinforcing its connection with such methodologies renders it more significant the agile paradigm is an additional natural inclusion to the project management practices for some professional that allow its widespread implementations due to the conformity with already used techniques.

Common pain points in the tech industry are emphasized with high efficiency and prioritization of approach, thereby attracting support from professionals who desire pragmatic solutions. Thus, through leading individuals towards what it vital for the current state and how to manage time, as well as streamline workflows, this paradigm becomes a strong tool in helping those managing tech projects deal with its fast pace and high stress nature.

Its use in all the spectrum of work such as management, manufacturers and customers makes it popular even more. Regardless of where one is at in development, project management, or even team leadership, the principles remain applicable. This universality helps to ensure that people performing different tasks within the realm of tech teams speak and understand the same language; hence, they all feel as one.

The socio-cultural context surrounding this paradigm places an emphasis on continuous improvement in a manner that resonates with the principles of constant learning and progressing skills that define tech environments. The approach is inherently synergetic and dynamic, reflecting the needs of professionals to keep-up with the latest technological advances while simultaneously striving for individual and collective development.

As we move along, the story goes beyond common limits, incorporating the technical with the psychological. The book utilizes both dynamics my dual professional identity as Coach and Psychologist presenting a humanistic element in professional relations. The integration seeks to arm the readers with a broad, yet potent arsenal of skills that they need to find their way through one of the most diverse industries out there.

Throughout the chapters, the tone is impartial and contentless, free of flourishes or needless sentimentality. This article aims to provide a practical real-life guidance applicable among professionals with diverse backgrounds despite have no knowledge about the complexity of coding.

In essence, this book is a practical manual full of the findings that the crossroads of technology and human behavior are always dynamic. What is behind this goal other than providing the knowledge is not to make ordinary readers gain a nuanced understanding but give them skills that help them understand changes occurring in tech markets.

Principle 0. Paradigm Shift in Tech

Hey there! In the constantly changing world of technology, we are about to set out on a path that is going to shake things up. Strap yourself in and brace for impact. Just think of this chapter as a ticket to the hottest show in town, with people backstage focusing not so much on lines of code but even more importantly trying the spotlight elsewhere – soft skills.

Now, let's set the stage. Just imagine a picture of the tech industry – a world once ruled by supreme mastery over technology. This is a world where the only true celebrities have been coding languages, algorithms and frameworks. But hey, we understand. Technical skill is the flesh and blood of this digital age – the sudsless heroes behind each app you've ever swiped, clicked or tapped on your mobile device. I think we are overdue for a shift in our paradigm, a seismic shake-up of traditional perceptions about success. The old belief that technical know-how is the key to success, deserves a critical examination. This is what we're all about – highlighting the soft skills, those unsung heroes.

What's more, a rumor has been circulating in the halls of technology that points out something new – the game is changing. But now it's not enough to just write good code. What's most important is how you cooperate, communicate and guide. That's about a spirit of all-roundness which is not simply technical.

So, here's the deal: we're flipping the script. What we're doing is defining success in tech by emphasizing soft skills. This is not a denying of technical strength; it's rather the upgrading, a high-tech movement where hard skills over soft skills and vice versa – both are exploding talents with divine harmony.

Thus, in this chapter we are providing the foundation. We'll play it through to the second era of this information technology landscape, where technical skills reigned supreme. So, we will illuminate the traditional focus on bits and bytes, because there's no denying that such skills are valuable. However, and here's the big condition. We will also be introducing paradigm change – change toward a Tech Culture that values soft skills as much or more than strong ones.

We are in the middle of a paradigm shift and preparing to rewrite the rules for tech. It's time to prepare. Take the plunge into a realm where success is no longer built around code but how you cooperate, communicate and adapt to this constantly shifting battlefield of technological advancement. This marks the start of something great. Here begins the new era of tech!

Let's now get to the crux of what we are talking about - how soft skills can be such a critical ingredient in tech. Strap in and prepare for the ride as we discover that there's often more to tech products than meets the eye. Picture this: you aren't just sitting in some dimly lit room, pounding out line after brilliant line. No, you are a tech virtuoso conducting the symphony of success and soft skills is your repertoire.

In this tech carnival, therefore, why are soft skills the VIP pass? Let's use some real-life examples to paint the picture. Consider the legendary tech project that not only met deadlines but exceeded them. What fueled that success? Not only was it the lines of code, but also, it's about a team working seamlessly together and communicating effectively to fight their way clear through that storm.

Soft skills are the lifeblood that binds up this tech tapestry. Picture the coder who not only produces squeaky-clean code, but communicates his ideas clearly, understands how others feel and click with them like a conductor. But wait, there's more! Soft skills aren't just about making the workplace feel like one big family (though that's nice, too). They're the things that will launch your career rocket into orbit. Picture this: It's not that you are going up the ladder of success; it is more like riding a high-rise elevator, powered by most equal proportions of technical ability and delicate finesse.

Let's break it down. Soft skills aren't a sidekick. They are the superhero cape that propel your tech flight into godhood status. They're the secret sauce that turns a good coder into an outstanding leader, dependable colleague and multi-problem solver. Success isn't in what you code alone. That's all about soft skills that enhance your greatness.

Upon looking at the evolving tech environment in view of the paradigm shift, we discover problems connected with historically not enough emphasis on soft skills. Can you picture going through a tech take-off with everything quite normal - the code is fine; the algorithm could not be better - when all sudden turbulence shakes up your comfortable flight?

Foremost among these challenges is the communication conundrum. Imagine what it would be like if fantastic ideas were lost in a clamor of tech gibberish unable to communicate. One can feel the tension involved in communicating ideas precisely, and this presents an obstacle to smooth cooperation.

As we spin through the maze of technology, crossing that chasm is no easy task. But what if a team is called the Dream Team, but cooperation like putting together jigsaw puzzle without any order. With no soft skills, projects fall by the wayside and deadlines turn white with panic. The dream team becomes a divided one indeed.

Throw in a bit of leadership drama. Imagine an effort directed by a code master but condemned because of managerial babble. This leads to chaos - an example of the leadership problem, in which a lack of soft skills turns a technological genius into a project's weakness. We are not trying to dissuade you from the tech roller-coaster; it is only a lighting of issues requiring confrontation. These are the real-world stories that convey case studies and anecdotes to guide us through some messy projects. soft skills have temporarily been cast aside. But these stories are no horror tales. Instead, they guide us, ever so cautiously, on our ride through the turns of the tech rollercoaster.

While the paradigm shift is still underway, we focus on a practical example that has emerged - case studies showing how incorporating soft skills into tech produces solid achievements. Over and above theory, these narratives provide concrete examples of tech companies or professionals that have bridged the gap between technical know-how and soft skills.

Such stories can't all be successful ones, but rather are proof that it really is possible to go through the tech maze with an integrated skill set. The strategies that were executed are also analyzed in terms of how the introduction of soft skills improved team relationships and co-operation for better outcome.

See the paradigm shift In this broad environment, let us examine a basic principle - The Proactive Mindset. Today, we explore the idea of proactivity in communications among tech teams. What's most important is not merely meeting the challenge, but to stay ahead of it - to see opportunity as well and gather people together for action.

Principle 1. Be Proactive in Communication

Chapter 1. The Foundation of Success: Proactive Communication in Tech

As we step into Principle 1: Communication among people is of the utmost importance. Our Be Proactive system opens the door to a world in which others are not simply being responsive, but participating creatively to achieve innovation and success. In tech teams, proactive communication is like a beautifully choreographed symphony. Even before the conductor's cues, each instrument plays its part in rhythm with everything else. The kind that you have to do on purpose - anticipate obstacles, seek opportunities and be proactive about participating in the group knowledge pool.

But in a fast-moving tech world, where the environment is constantly changing and has no place for sluggards, bold communication upon serious introspection also marks their pulse of development. What I mean is that it's not only about the flow of information, but also building an atmosphere in which everyone feels comfortable freely contributing to tell a larger story together.

What if tech professionals didn't just wait for the next update, but rather went seeking information? If not a reactive process and passive waiting, then by being anticipatory exchanges of creative work. This attitude of taking the initiative in communication stimulates this culture of constant renewal and reformation.

In this chapter we have analyses the complex nature of proactive communication and unraveled its many hidden meanings. More than just a list of actions, it is an attitude - a desire to be constantly ahead of the game; understanding where things are headed next and doing one's part in the interactive exchange. We examine the spirit of proactive communication in tech and take a tour into the future to reshape how our teams interact, communicate, share ideas, and build momentum towards success. This is the age of active communication in technology, where initiative will be key to success.

Chapter 2. The Impact of Proactive Communication

In the continuum of Principle 1: Proactive Communication, we continue exploring the deep influence that proactive communication can have on another aspect of tech life - group interactions. In this chapter, we explore how the active exchange of ideas, thoughts and information gives teamwork a different texture. In essence, proactive communication is a catalyst for team synergy. It goes beyond the relationship of information transfer, creating an environment where everyone's intelligence is shared and utilized proactively. With everyone taking the initiative to speak out and anticipate possible obstacles, team relationships can undergo a transformation.

Picture a team that communicates not merely to report on progress, but has developed active initial communication which foresees problems and works as a coherent whole. The effect is enormous - it creates a culture of mutual responsibility, in which members are willing to offer ideas and observations.

In this chapter, we examine a few real-world situations where proactive communication has been the key to effective teamwork. But we chose to see just how successful such a proactive mindset can be. Can it make tech teams work more effectively together and as limits approached?

What's more, we explain the concept of Proactive 'Techversations' - discussions that go beyond exchanging information. These tech talks turn into opportunities for mutual understanding, teamwork and a desire to get the job done right. While we explore the effect of this proactive communication, imagine a group where everyone actively helps - not to react by getting things under control but rather as an effort created in pursuit of excellence. Man has always been a social animal. The pot individuals can have on each other depends upon how they choose communicating with others, and this chapter is about the influence proactive communication will exert in teams of all activities future happiness or failure resting atop its shoulders. Ready yourself to watch the power of proactive communication at work shaping this delicate interplay between teams in technology.

See if you can imagine a tech company where active interaction is not something to be ticked as completed but instead becomes part of the project ethic. Such success stories are like lighthouses, showing us the way to a future in which such active communication isn't merely an option; it is a prerequisite if we want to achieve the full potential of tech projects.

Chapter 3. Barriers to Proactive Communication in Tech

As we continue our exploration of Principle 1: Obstacles and Indicators we then turn our lens on the technical environment, focusing instead upon obstacles to successful proactive communication. But this chapter takes us on a thought – provoking trip through the potholes and perceptions that hinder their passage, as well as how to get past them.

The time crunch Let us first focus on an issue that is shared by many, one which stems from the lightning-quick world of tech today. With cramped schedules and heavy workloads, team members usually view proactive communication as yet another hassle. It's a misconception to suppose that proactive communication is time-consuming.

Second, the tech industry use of virtual communications tools can end up making a connection more difficult. But team members may be reluctant to start up digital chatting of their own accord, afraid that they will misunderstand or underestimate each other. The problem is to find a balance between convenience and the other tool, open communication.

There are also cultural problems brought on by the silo effect of individual specialist cultures. The difficulty is figuring out how to get past these silos and have everyone work together as a team.

Now, let's explore misconceptions. A few might say that initiating communication is meant for leaders or specially – assigned liaisons, but does not apply to collective responsibility uniting the whole team. Breaking this myth requires rewriting the story to focus on how people of all levels should be developing active communication.

In this issue, we'll look into how to break down these obstacles. We will examine everything from time management methods to creation of an atmosphere conducive for open communication in tech, offering concrete suggestions on how everyone can break down these barriers and establish a new culture of aggressive action.

This is not simply a list of problems, but also the road through and around them. In the process of breaking down these enclosures, visualize a technology environment in which difficulties become resources for creativity and cooperation. Prepare to tear down the barriers and encourage an environment of vigorous communication.

Chapter 4. Mastering the Art: Developing Proactive Communication Skills in Tech

As we go through these easy steps and activities, imagine a world full of technology where good communication is not just something you can do but it's like an important talent. This chapter is your tool for learning how to write messages well in tech. It will help you become better at working together with a team and making new ideas happen.

Now, we'll leave theory and move to the practice – active interaction in this changing technology world. The point of this chapter is to provide practical steps and drills that allow technology folk themselves to become expert practitioners of proactive communication.

1. **Embrace Digital Tools Mindfully:** Select communication tools that complement proactive engagement. Utilize features like status updates and channels dedicated to discussions, ensuring a balance between efficiency and open communication.

2. **Set Communication Goals:** Define specific communication objectives for yourself and the team. Whether it's initiating a certain number of „Techversations" per week or sharing insights on project progress, setting goals fosters a proactive mindset.

3. **Active Listening Exercises:** Engage in active listening exercises during team meetings or discussions. Practice paraphrasing and summarizing to ensure a thorough understanding of others' perspectives before contributing your insights.

4. **Proactive 'Techversations':** Initiate proactive 'Techversations' by posing open-ended questions related to ongoing projects or potential challenges. Encourage team members to share insights and collectively brainstorm solutions.

5. **Time Management Techniques:** Implement time management strategies to allocate dedicated slots for proactive communication. This ensures that it becomes an integral part of your daily routine without overwhelming your schedule.

6. **Feedback Loops:** Establish feedback loops within the team. Encourage regular feedback on communication styles, ensuring that constructive insights contribute to the continuous improvement of proactive communication practices.

7. **Cultivate a Growth Mindset:** Foster a mindset of continuous improvement. Embrace challenges as opportunities to enhance your communication skills and adapt to evolving team dynamics.

8. **Cross-Functional Collaboration Exercises:** Engage in cross-functional collaboration exercises where tech professionals from different departments collaborate on simulated projects. This enhances adaptability and proactive communication across diverse roles.

The following situations and pretend games are useful for computer experts to practice active talking in a make - believe but real place. When people join in these tasks, they not only learn the rules of active talk but also take them to heart by using them for real.

- **Scenario 1**: Picture a situation where the project halts and people on team don't want to say their worries out loud. In this pretend game, people play different team parts and talk about possible problems. The goal is to make people in the team talk more, so they feel strong and can share ideas together. This helps everyone find answers as a group.

- **Scenario 2**: The Techversation Initiative - in this situation, the group is changing to a forward-thinking way of talking. People join in a game where they start talking about technology and projects that are happening now. The goal is to practice asking smart questions, really hearing answers and adding important ideas in the talk.

- **Scenario 3**: Imagine a situation where different tech teams have to work together on a project. In an exercise where people pretend to be in different departments, they take on roles and learn how to work together. This situation shows how important it is to change the way we talk in order to work well together with people from different jobs.

- **Scenario 4**: In this activity, people act out giving and receiving feedback quickly so they can learn from each other. This situation is about two teammates talking about a recent project. One person gives good advice and the other gets it. The aim is to grow a way of sharing open feedback and always getting better.
- **Scenario 5**: Time Use Problem: In this real-life situation, people take on a time management challenge where they must include active communication into their everyday schedules. By doing pretend games, people deal with their tasks and make time for helpful talking. They also get past obstacles that have to do with how much time they have.

This part will help you get better at talking before problems happen. It does this by putting you in real-life situations and practicing with different roles to play. Prepare to act like a good talker and see how these methods change things.

Chapter 5. Active Participation: Fun Activities for Learning Effective Communication Skills.

In the culmination of Principle 1, get involved in talking, this part is more than just reading it. It's also a fun and exciting experience. In a series of activities, readers are asked to use and learn active ways to communicate. These methods turn what they know into skills they can do actively.

1. Start a **7-day Techversation Challenge**. Start a tech talk in your team or with other staff each day. Set the conversation going, don't just wait for it to happen! Share knowledge, ask questions that can be answered in more than just simple ways and promote a chat that moves past everyday reports. Think about how these talks affect working together and sharing of knowledge.

2. Create a **Proactive Mindset Journal**. During a week, write down times when you spoke up early or saw someone else doing it. Think about the problems you faced and how things turned out positively. Use this diary to keep getting better all the time.

3. **Participate in pretending games** about tech projects. Do different jobs on a team and talk about possible problems, creative fixes, and ways to work together. Think about how good communication helps make these pretend situations better.

4. **Time Management** for Proactive Communication. Make a plan to manage your time better for active communication. Set aside time in your schedule for active conversation tasks like starting tech talk or giving out ideas. Think about how useful this method is for including active talking in your everyday life.

5. **Proactive Feedback Exchange**. Start a helpful talk about how things are going with someone at work. Work on giving helpful advice for a recent work or job, focus on showing how early talks help make progress better all the time. Think about how this sharing of thoughts affects your teamwork.

When you do these activities, imagine a friendly talking trip that's more than just learning. This part is your guide for real-world practice – a big change where understanding meets doing. Prepare yourself to jump into active talking, where each practice helps you improve in the fast tech communication area.

Think about how you talk now, find places where being more active can be improved. Check how comfortable you are with starting talks about technology, giving helpful feedback before asked and actively joining in team discussions. Think about old projects where good communication was very important. Find examples where taking action from the start made good results in working together, solving problems or finishing projects. Use these thoughts to help you make goals that are best for yourself.

Make clear goals to start 'Techversations' actively. Tell how often and what kind of these talks happen, thinking about both group and personal situations. Set clear goals to see how you're doing and celebrate successes when making a mindset for better communication.

Start a helpful feedback process in your team or work group. Ask for comments on how you talk and try to learn about places where you can get better. Use this advice as a base for making focused goals to improve your active talking skills.

Make a constant getting better notebook just for your active talk trip. Keep a diary of your experiences, issues and victories when using active talk methods daily. Use this diary to think about yourself and change your goals for ongoing betterment.

As you go through this stage, think of talking to others not just as a talent but also as your promise for self-improvement. This helps you learn more about yourself and get strong. It's an amazing experience where checking yourself becomes the guide, and making plans works as a map for your trek in mastering good communication skills by being active with it. Prepare to start improving constantly and see your active talking skills grow in the busy world of tech communication.

Chapter 6. Building a Proactive Communication Culture

In the final exploration of Principle 1 this chapter talks about the important task of making sure tech teams and companies have a good approach to talking with each other. It's called building proactive communication culture. It is more than just what a person can do, and looks at ways that everyone in the group uses. In this change of culture, leadership is very important for encouraging people to talk freely.

Look at a big set of methods made to put in active talking into the core stuff of tech groups. Talk about setting up regular tech talks, making special places for free conversation, and putting in a system to give direct comments. These plans make up the foundation for a society where talking isn't just needed, but it is actively and together done.

In the world of leaders helping to make open talk happen, leaders are those who build a setting where first-rate communication and sharing can grow. They start the conversation by taking part in talks, starting open chats and showing weakness when they share their thoughts. Making a place where people can speak their thoughts and worries without being scared of punishment is very important in good leadership. Letting team members share their ideas and getting input from everyone helps to build a good way of talking. This is called proactive communication culture.

Leadership means giving useful advice that motivates people to talk openly. When bosses encourage positive talk, they help make it normal for everyone on the team. Setting up special talking spaces like team meetings or forums helps workers to share ideas and talk about problems.

Leaders are very important in making sure that talking to each other before things happen becomes a basic belief within the team. Being responsible is also important, where team members are asked to participate and help in proactive talking efforts. Changing leadership styles to match good communication rules makes talking in a team better.

Basically, Leadership's Role in Promoting Open Dialogue is about making a place where all team members feel important and understood. It's about building a style where creativity, teamwork and victory are normal results of active talk that includes everyone.

In dealing with problems, leaders are very important in taking an active step forward. Instead of thinking about problems as barriers, leadership helps the team recognizing and taking care of them directly. This active approach means making a space where team members can freely talk about worries, share ideas and work together to find answers. The team works on problems to make things better all the time, strong and able to change.

Just as important is the active congratulation of successes, whether they are big or small. Leaders guide in noticing and confirming accomplishments that match the targets of a group or company. This party is not just a show but an intentional step to emphasize good actions and results. When leaders show and praise successes, it creates a good circle of encouragement. This helps to keep the team members excited and inspired by what they do. It makes a society where successes are not just marks, but sparkers for persistent greatness.

Basically, tackling problems and praising accomplishments are part of the same active approach. Leaders help the team face problems with strength and cleverness. At the same time, they make sure that every win is noticed and enjoyed. This two-way method makes the base of an active talking way where team lives on handling problems and enjoying their wins.

This part will help the bosses, teammates and those who shape an organization learn together how to improve a good talking culture. This is a look into ways, how to lead others and also match with people's culture that will make tech teams work better together. This stuff leads them down a new path of success. Prepare to promote the active communication habit that changes teams and groups into successful places of creativity and free talk.

Principle 2. Begin with the End in Mind

Chapter 1. Setting the Stage - Tech Leadership

As we embark on the exploration of Principle 2: Start with the End in Mind (Leadership for Tech) is the opening chapter. It studies how leadership works and its effects within changing tech world.

Being a leader in the tech world is more than just following old ways. It is the leading light that helps companies navigate through technology's complex and always changing landscape. This part aims to understand what leadership is about. It goes beyond just managing things and reveals a role that involves planning, seeing the future clearly and connecting it with how new ideas are made.

In this easy start, we explore the difficult parts of saying what leadership means in tech. It's more than just a job; it's the designer of future where technology isn't simply used but fully tapped. Leaders help to make places where new ideas don't just happen sometimes but are part of the culture in a group.

The tech world, full of quick changes and big shifts marked by constant challenges needs leaders who handle these obstacles with a vision for the future. In this part, we look at how leaders are very important in making the atmosphere for company culture. They also make places where imagination grows and people feel strong enough to be all they can be.

Leading in tech is more than just managing a project. It changes groups into part of a common dream, motivating them to beat usual limits. Leaders support success in groups, making sure everyone shares the same goal that is more than just personal tasks.

When we look at leadership in tech, imagine a place where leaders decidedly control the direction of technology. This part is ready to start a big change. Here, being in charge isn't just about choosing between two things but becomes the reason that makes new ideas last longer and growth happen together all the time in our growing tech world.

In the changing world of tech leaders, making a plan and being ready for what comes is very important to doing well. This understanding shows how important leaders are in guiding the constantly changing technology world.

A strong idea is like the leader, directing teams and projects. It goes beyond everyday jobs and offers a group reason, connecting people towards the same target. A clear vision is not just a fixed idea; it's an active force that makes new ideas happen, brings people together and gives each team member direction.

Along with the need for a view, we also require an active leadership style. In the fast-moving world of technology, it's not just good to be ready for change. It is essential. Leaders who act ahead of time watch for changes in technology. They see change as a way to get better and prepare their teams so they can keep up with what's happening around them. This method is more than just responding to problems; it's about making the future happen, moving forward with new ideas and setting up a stronger chance of lasting success.

In times of uncertainty, a clear vision becomes something that brings stability. It gives a guide for making choices, showing what to do when things are not clear. Leaders who take action can move through uncertainties easily. They use a clear picture of the future to make decisions and do things right. They don't just react to change; they actively help make it happen based on their big picture.

Good leadership always comes with a bit of inspiring. Good leaders that clearly share their vision with enthusiasm and realness get their people to do more than they ever have before. In this situation, good leadership means making a place where team members are not just people who help but those who actively work to make the vision we all share come true. It helps create a system where new ideas are not just one-off things but always developing. This happens because everyone wants to reach the future we have imagined together.

It is important to stress the need for a plan and active leadership style. This means finding just right balance between things. It's about showing a strong picture while being fast and able to react when the tech world changes. Vision gives us where to go, and being active makes sure we can change and bounce back as things keep changing.

In other words, tech leaders who know the value of a clear goal and take action are ready to help their teams face problems, grab chances and make greatness in always changing technology world.

Chapter 2. The Visionary Leader in Tech

In the complex world of tech leadership, it's very important to be a visionary leader. A good boss in the tech world isn't just a task supervisor but also an encourager for change and creativity.

A good leader in tech has qualities that go beyond what people usually think of as leadership. It is about making a strong vision and being able to tell it. This goes beyond the current problems or future plans. Leaders with good ideas can see into the future. They know what new tech trends are coming and imagine a time when their teams will be important in deciding how technology develops.

Visionary leadership in tech focuses on being able to change and adjust. The always changing way of technology needs leaders who can handle uncertainties quickly and strong. Great leaders don't run away from change. They love it and use each change to help their groups get closer to the future they see.

Talking is a big part of being a great leader. Tech leaders need to explain their vision clearly, with emotion and honesty. The power to encourage and push team members relies on the leader's skill in showing how important it is for our future goal. Great leaders make everyone agree, helping all to be committed together for big goals.

Visionary leadership in tech comes with a built-in tendency to innovate. People who lead this way always look for ways to make new ideas and improve technology. They promote a place where imagination grows, helping people in the group to think past usual limits.

Collaboration is another vital quality. Great leaders know that working together is important to get the future they want. They make places that help different ideas and build teamwork with people who have various skills or backgrounds.

Finally, a good leader in tech helps everyone succeed by making sure each member shares the same goal. They do more than just handle tasks; they encourage greatness and develop a joint promise to reach new levels in the constantly changing tech world. On the path of Principle 2, plans for exciting leadership help push tech teams towards a future with great innovation and teamwork. This makes winning not just something they want but part of their story itself in technology world.

Good tech leadership starts with a clear vision. Many examples show that tech leaders have followed this visionary way, guiding their companies to great success.

One great example is Steve Jobs, who started Apple Inc. with his friends. Ricky was famous for knowing what people wanted and changing businesses to better suit them. His idea for easy-to-use and good-looking products changed Apple into a big tech company that always tried new ways of being inventive.

Elon Musk, the boss of Tesla and SpaceX, is another good example. Musk's big thinking goes past his plans for clean energy and space travel. His clear idea for electric cars and space travel has not only changed businesses but also inspired a new time of tech chances.

Satya Nadella, the boss of Microsoft, shows more examples of great leadership in tech world. With his help, Microsoft changed its direction towards cloud computing and artificial intelligence. He made the company match well with how technology is changing nowadays.

These leaders have a similar idea - they started with an obvious picture that went beyond short-term problems. Their power to talk about and work towards an exciting future made it possible for big change. They saw things differently. With their smart ideas, they didn't just deal with the hard parts of tech work but also helped decide where it would go next.

Great leaders in tech don't just follow what others are doing; they imagine and build a future that some might not yet understand. Their ability to motivate, create new ideas and guide with a goal shows how strong it is starting by knowing the end result. In a changing world of technology, these leaders show the way for their groups. They point to the future with ideas and long-lasting victories based on great thoughts and progress.

Chapter 3. Setting Long-Term Goals

In the fast-moving world of technology, it's really important to set goals for a long time. This idea is the map that helps tech bosses go through the changing and unexpected areas of this job.

Long-term goals give a plan for making decisions and sharing out resources. They act like the North Star, guiding teams in one direction and creating a shared goal. In the fast-changing tech world, where trends can quickly change, having long-term goals gives a strong base. This helps keep things steady and moving in one direction during changes.

Creating goals for the future is not just about making plans, it's also about actively changing what happens. Tech bosses who use this idea are builders of their company's future. They see a future where their products, services and ideas help make technology stories important.

It's even more important to have long-term goals when new technologies or changes in the market happen. Groups that make big, smart goals are in a better place to handle problems, change quickly and take new chances. Long-term goals help tech leaders go beyond short-term changes and focus on the lasting effect they want to have.

Moreover, these aims create an environment where new ideas and constant improvement are encouraged. They make teams want to go beyond limits, try new tech stuff and stay in front of what's happening. Long-term goals help businesses be more creative. They make them think about the future and how to change in a way that helps them succeed long term too.

Basically, making long-term goals in the fast-changing tech world is a good plan that helps leaders deal with uncertainties and keep winning success over time. It changes how businesses work, from reacting to changing things on purpose. This makes sure they stay ahead in a world where technology keeps changing all the time.

In the constantly changing world of leading tech companies, knowing how to set long-term goals is not just a smart plan; it's an action that leads businesses towards lasting success. To share their vision well, leaders in technology need a group of ways to plan that go beyond the normal range for setting targets.

1. **Clarity and Simplicity**: The first plan is to turn the vision into a clear and easy-to-understand story. Tech bosses need to clearly say their big plans in a way that all inside and outside people can easily understand. Clear understanding makes sure everyone agrees, helping to create a shared view of the future.

2. **Aligning with Core Values**: A good plan is one that agrees with the important beliefs of the group. Tech bosses should mix the big aims smoothly into their firm's purpose and beliefs. This

matching not only makes the vision real but also gives team members a sense of meaning.

3. **Inclusivity and Collaboration**: Working together is important when making long-term goals. Leaders in tech should include important people when they make their plans. They need to ask for ideas and learn from different viewpoints. Being fair and including everyone adds depth to the big picture. It also builds a shared responsibility that pushes all of the group together for their common aim.

4. **Visual Communication**: Images can be strong ways to share an idea. Tech leaders should use pictures like charts, diagrams or infographics to show the big goals for a long time. Seeing pictures helps us understand better and keeps the imagined future fresh in our minds.

5. **Storytelling**: Making a strong story for long-term goals is very important. Tech leaders should tell stories to explain the path, problems and victories linked with their vision. A well-told story connects with the people, making them feel something strong. This increases their dedication and excitement.

6. **Adaptability and Iteration**: A vision is not a fixed thing; it changes with the shifting world of technology. Tech bosses should accept changing and improvement in their long-term plans. Check and change the vision often based on what's happening, how technology is improving, or when your company grows.

7. **Continuous Communication**: Good talking is always happening. Tech bosses should keep talking all the time about their big future plans, share news and learnings. They need to celebrate success too. Regular talk helps to keep the dream going. It makes sure that it stays a helpful power in what an organization does every day.

In short, making long-term plans in the tech field is a complex job that needs clever thinking and imaginative ideas. Clear plans, staying on track together, teamwork visually showing stories that can change make a beautiful picture. This will bring goals to life in an exciting way when we keep talking and adapting all the time.

If this idea is made clear and shared well, it turns into a guiding light for the whole company. It offers guidance, meaning and a joint goal. Long-term goals are more than just a big plan. They become an exciting story that pushes teams to move forward, sparking new ideas and teamwork while making everyone tough when technology changes.

Tech leaders start setting big goals for the future. They're very focused on moving forward at every step, and their destination is not just a place far away but something that affects how businesses grow over time. The ideas of simple, matching actions, working together and use clear communicating should be our guide. This helps make sure that the future we want is not just a place to go but something everyone does. It drives success in fast-changing technology world by being an agreement from all sides on what goal we need achieved as teamwork matters more than individual efforts or own advantage with sales boost up locally before Long-term goals are very important in technology and leadership. They can change things, start new ideas, and show how powerful visionary leaders can be.

Chapter 4. Empowering Tech Teams

In the world of tech leaders, power is a key idea that helps companies move towards their dream future. This part looks at the close connection between good leadership and giving power to tech groups. It shows how big leaders are very important in making a place where people can do well on their own or as teams.

Good leadership in the tech world is more than just regular bosses. It means making a place where everyone on the team can share their special skills and ideas freely. This idea is not the same for everyone; it's about understanding and helping different skills in a tech team.

Basically, giving power to tech teams means offering freedom and tools needed for creativity to grow. Leaders who think big know that being creative isn't a straight path. It needs surroundings where people feel strong to take chances, discover new thoughts and question the usual way of doing things.

Talking becomes very important in making people feel strong. Tech bosses who make a clear plan, keep realistic hopes and listen well to their groups build an open culture based on trust. In that kind of place, team members feel strong to speak their minds, express worries and take part actively in the big aim.

Giving power to tech groups also means creating a place where people can learn. In the always changing tech world, keep learning isn't just a choice; it is needed. Great leaders spend on making their groups better. They give chances to learn new skills, know more things and grow in jobs. This dedication to learning gives people power and also makes sure the whole team can change together.

Recognition and admittance are very important for giving power. Good leaders know how important it is to celebrate success, whether big or small. Seeing how hard tech teams work and their successes not only makes them happy but also helps build pride in own work.

Also, giving power means making a fair space where different views are not just accepted but really looked for. Leaders who think big know the power of a group with different experiences, skills and backgrounds. Inclusivity helps create a lot of fresh ideas, pushing the team towards smart answers.

This part looks at how good leadership, based on starting with the end goal in mind makes technology teams stronger. Good leaders create places where people can learn continuously and act together to share a goal. They do this by giving power, being clear about what they say, always trying new ways and showing appreciation for their efforts in working fairly with everyone. Giving power to groups who work with computers is not only a plan by bosses; it's about letting every person use all their ability together for the shared future of machines. These actions pushed them forward to amazing new ideas and inventions in the world of tech.

Sundar Pichai - Google: As Google's top boss, Sundar Pichai has been a big part in creating an environment of power and invention. Pichai leads his teams by promoting creativity and letting them be independent. By supporting big projects like Google's self-driving cars and efforts in artificial intelligence, Pichai has built a place where people feel strong to make the most of technology.

Shantanu Narayen - Adobe: Shantanu Narayen, the head of Adobe, is another great leader who supports giving power. Narayan has created an environment that encourages trying new things and learning from mistakes. Narayen has given resources for learning and made ways to talk openly. This helps Adobe's tech teams work on new ideas in design, multimedia and digital experiences.

Tim Cook - Apple: Tim Cook, the boss of Apple, has kept up the tradition started by Steve Jobs for creating new things. Cook's way of leading focuses on teamwork and letting everyone in. It encourages Apple's tech groups to work together well so they can finish big projects first. The introduction of things like the Apple Watch and changing Macs to use Apple's own computer parts shows how empowered we were under Cook.

Satya Nadella - Microsoft: Satya Nadella, the boss of Microsoft, has helped make the firm better by focusing on giving people power and being open to everyone. Under Nadella's direction, Microsoft has taken on a mindset for growth. They motivate people to learn and test things all the time. This change in culture has given tech teams the power to lead new things like cloud computing, artificial intelligence and mixed reality.

Elon Musk - Tesla and SpaceX: Elon Musk's leadership at Tesla and SpaceX shows dedication to helping others do more things in new ways. Musk often gets his groups to work on big projects like electric cars, renewable energy and space travel. By making a place where taking risks is good and learning from mistakes is welcomed, Musk has helped tech teams to make great progress.

These bosses have one thing in common - they know that real new ideas come when people feel powerful to think freely, take chances and share their special opinions. These tech bosses have made their teams strong and able. By doing that, they got them to think about what the future might bring while keeping goal in mind from start of it all. By doing this, they not only reached big tech goals but also built a history of stronger teams constantly working to improve things.

Chapter 5. Overcoming Leadership Challenges in Tech

Tech leaders face many problems that are normal in their industry. These problems, even though different from each other, have similarities. They need a plan to guide companies so they can reach their imagined goals in the future.

First of all, the fast rate at which technology changes gives a constant problem. To stay ahead, leaders need to be active and always watch for new trends. They should make learning a never-ending thing in their group of workers.

Keeping skilled workers is a big problem because lots of tech jobs need these people. Bosses need to focus on creating work environments that value differences, include everyone and keep workers learning. This helps get the best people for jobs while keeping them there.

Leaders need to set up flexible company systems and rules that carefully balance new ideas with keeping things steady. Making a culture that allows trying new things within limits makes sure there's balance between growth and keeping safe.

Working together across different fields is another hard part as technology gets more and more linked. Leaders should make different fields work together, connecting technical and non-technical groups to help solve bigger problems in a whole way.

Leaders must always make cybersecurity a top priority because there's always danger from hacking. They need to plan ahead against it. This means putting strong safety steps in place, checking them often and teaching teams about the best ways to protect important information.

Technology progress makes us face big problems in right and social sense. Leaders need to deal with these ethical thoughts by making rules and talking in a real way with people involved, so they can develop technology carefully. Developing leaders in the fast-changing tech world is always needed. Leaders should put money into projects, help from older people and training to make their abilities better. They also need knowledge about the newest things happening in that area of work.

To beat these problems, you need a complete plan. This should use active ways to fix issues and make the workplace happy place for employees as well as flexible designs that help growth run smoothly together with people from different types of work, good security online protection measures too, be ethical about it all couple this effort up by keeping your leaders improving constantly. If tech bosses handle these issues carefully, they can help their companies reach a future full of new ideas and triumphs.

Leading in tech world needs a full and smart plan. Here's an integrated set of insights and solutions to overcome each challenge:

- **Rapid Technological Changes**: Encourage a mindset of always learning in the team. Set up regular learning sessions, promote getting certificates and make ways for sharing knowledge. This helps the team be up-to-date with changing technologies, promoting flexibility and creativity.

- **Talent Acquisition and Retention**: Make it a top goal to create good office habits that appreciate differences, welcome everyone and help professionals improve. Provide good pay packages, make chances for better jobs and set up guide programs. This makes it easier to get and keep the best workers.

- **Balancing Innovation with Stability**: Build a flexible organization that can easily change when needed. Use methods like Agile and DevOps to find a balance between promoting creativity and keeping things steady. Promote an environment where experiments happen within certain limits to push for new ideas.

- **Interdisciplinary Collaboration**: Accept different ideas and knowledge in the group. Help form teams from different areas, promote open talking and organize gatherings with people from many fields. This encourages working together and sharing knowledge, connecting teams that are good with technology to those who aren't.

- **Cybersecurity Threats**: Choose a strong cybersecurity plan by spending on good safety steps. Do regular checks, teach people about good ways to keep their computers safe all the time and create a mindset of always being careful. This makes sure that private information stays safe from growing dangers.

- **Ethical and Social Implications**: Recognize and deal with the moral and social effects of new technology. Create easy rules that are always right, talk honestly with people involved to learn their worries and make laws for using technology well. This makes sure technology is created and used the right way.

By using these ideas and answers in their way of leading, tech leaders can face problems well. They help make new things creative and guide companies to keep doing good work for a long time while technology keeps changing all the time.

Chapter 6. Examples of Developing Leadership Skills

Satya Nadella, the current CEO of Microsoft, presents a compelling case study of a tech leader who meticulously honed his skills over time. Nadella's trip began in 1992 when he joined Microsoft. By always learning and changing the way you lead, he went on to be CEO by 2014. Nadella's first efforts highlighted his vision and flexibility. He was very important in helping Microsoft create their cloud services. He saw that the industry needed to move towards computing done on clouds. His early understanding of tech changes showed he can change and create new things.

When Nadella became the boss of Microsoft, he started a big change in how people work there. He focused on teamwork, inclusion and always learning. He made the group feel strong and able to bounce back from challenges. This change in culture made workers see problems as chances to learn and get better.

His big plan was key to guide Microsoft for winning. He shared a simple plan, stressing the value of mobile and cloud tools. This changed Microsoft from a mainly Windows-centered company to one that accepts many devices and focuses on the cloud.

Nadella also put empathy first as a leader and worked on making strong teams. He focused on learning what employees and customers really needed. This helped create an environment that encourages new ideas and teamwork. This led to strong teams and a workplace where people felt confident in sharing their best thoughts.

The results of Nadella's leadership show a lot. Under his direction, Microsoft made a lot of money. The worth of the company increased more than three times during that time. The change in culture brought more teamwork and creativity. This is seen with the successful release of things like Azure, Office 365, buying LinkedIn too.

Basically, Satya Nadella's journey as a leader is an amazing example for people who want to lead in tech areas. His path shows how much learning all the time, changing to fit new things, planning well ahead and caring about others is needed in technology nowadays. It also points out that building a team sparks success within this field's ongoing changes.

The story of Tesla, led by imaginative businessman Elon Musk, shows a strong tale of a technology firm built on clear and big goals. Established in 2003, Musk's vision for Tesla was unequivocal: to speed up the shift of our world to green energy.

Musk's leadership was all about caring for the environment and thinking that electric cars could be really good. He imagined a future where electric cars became better, more efficient and popular than old gasoline vehicles. This idea prepared the way for Tesla's adventure into car making and clean energy industries.

Musk's leadership focused on being inventive and causing change. When Tesla brought out new electric cars like the Roadster, Model S and 3 made by Musk, it showed how much he cares about moving forward for electric vehicles. The big plan also had a part about controlling the whole production process. Tesla wanted to do it all themselves so they can work better and make sure everything is really good quality.

Beyond electric cars, Musk grew Tesla's goal to make an all-round clean energy world. This included buying SolarCity and creating storage energy products like Powerwall and Powerpack.

Musk's leadership at Tesla has had a big effect. People liked Tesla's electric cars a lot. They showed that electric vehicles can be useful and just as good as normal ones. The value of Tesla's company got really big, making it one of the most important car makers in the whole world. Moreover, Tesla's effect went past cars and started discussions about green energy. It also encouraged other businesses to put money in electric vehicle tech too.

In short, the Tesla study shows how a big and clear dream with smart leadership can bring powerful change in technology world. Elon Musk's constant dedication to keeping things green and making big changes puts Tesla as a leader in electric cars. They also work on clean energy options like solar power or windmills.

In the middle of Europe, Peter Wennink is a great leader. He leads ASML and helps to create new things in making tiny computer chips - known as semiconductors. As the boss of a Dutch company, Wennink leads clearly and shows how we can move forward with chip technology.

ASML is a world-wide top company in making machines for photolithography. It's very important technology used to make computer chips or semiconductors. Wennink's idea is about making new things in lithography for semiconductors. This helps to make small and strong microchips. With Wennink as the leader, ASML has been a strong user of new technology. They made special progress with extreme ultraviolet (EUV) lithography or microscopic picture making technique. This cool new tech has helped make small transistors, helping change semiconductor gadgets.

His big plan goes beyond just making technology. ASML works with chip makers around the world. This shows his dedication to building international teamwork for better industry progress. This view of everyone together makes ASML a big part in the world chip system.

Wennink, a European tech leader at ASML has not just made an impact on the company but also all of semiconductors. His leadership shows that European companies can lead new ideas in important tech areas. This proves leaders who are not from Silicon Valley also have a big impact on the global technology world.

In a nutshell, Peter Wennink's leadership at ASML shows that European leaders in the tech industry have great vision. His clear view, dedication to better technology and teamwork put ASML as an important part in deciding the future of chip making around world.

Chapter 7. Interactive Leadership Workshop and Practical Tips

In the Interactive Leadership Workshop, we start a hands-on study of leadership ideas just for tech leaders. This training is made to help readers use these ideas in their own leadership jobs or dreams, inside the fast tech world.

1. **Embrace Continuous Learning**: Develop a way of thinking that you always want to learn more by staying curious and looking for information. Make your own list of books to read that has leadership, company knowledge and successful stories. Go to online meetings, classes and events to learn more.
2. **Effective Communication**: Get better at talking by being easy to understand, quick and changing how you speak based on who is listening. Take part in chances to speak in public, like talking at team gatherings or business conventions. Practice making your

message more suitable for different groups of people and getting helpful tips to make it better.

3. **Emotional Intelligence**: Learn about feelings to handle friendships and know how a group works together. Do regular checks on your feelings and reactions in different situations. Practice understanding others by really listening to your team members and seeing things from their point of view.

4. **Decision-Making Skills**: Improve your choice-making by balancing thinking with making quick decisions. Take part in activities where you have to make decisions based on different situations. Look at possible results, think about dangers and make choices in a certain time. Look at the results and learn from both good things done right as well as tough situations faced.

5. **Team Building**: Build a good team spirit by creating trust and supporting working together. Set up team-building activities that suit different likes and abilities. Think about how your team works together and find ways to make it better. Promote talking freely in the group.

6. **Adaptability**: Learn to change and look for ways you can grow by accepting new things. Pretend different change situations like using new tools or organizing teams in a fresh way. Practice guiding your group through shifts and get advice on how well you adjust and communicate during change.

7. **Strategic Thinking**: Make a plan for success by matching your moves with big dreams that last. Engage in strategic planning sessions. Find main goals, look at market changes and create plans to act. Tell your team about the big plans you have, and ask for their ideas so that everyone can work together.

8. **Mentorship and Networking**: Look for help and make friends in your job to learn new things. Go to business events, talk with people on websites like LinkedIn and contact possible teachers. Join mentorship programs and look for chances to learn from others too.

9. **Self-Reflection**: Often think about your journey as a leader to make yourself more aware and grow. Save some time just for thinking about yourself. Write down your experiences, problems and wins. Find out what's good and bad, then make goals to keep getting better in leadership.

By doing these suggestions and exercises, make them a part of being a good leader. This will help you learn more skills and always try to do better which is needed for strong tech leadership.

People learn useful hints about their way of leading and what they need to improve. The aim is to help people feel sure, inventive and flexible as leaders in their tech jobs.

As we conclude our exploration of Principle 2: Start with the end in mind, this journey of visionary leadership begins on tech land. It shows how to plan well into the future and take important steps forward carefully.

By accepting this rule, we have explored the basic ideas of being a leader that go beyond just problems in tech. Leaders who start their jobs with a clear plan and focus on long-term goals have shown how they can change things.

The stories of leaders like Elon Musk, Steve Jobs and Safra Catz show the real results that happen when they start on their travels with a clear place to reach in mind. These bosses have done amazing things like changing electric cars, making new ideas for users better and dealing with the hard bits of big tech companies. They helped a lot because they knew what their goal was from the start.

As tech leaders, we are builders of the future and this idea asks us to wear a visionary hat. It asks us to say what we want in the future, not just as dreams but like lights showing our choices and how we work out plans. The idea asks us to look past the nearby view, imagining how our leadership could affect businesses, neighborhoods and even the whole world.

In simple terms, "Start with the End in Mind" means we should think carefully about our use of technology. This includes making sure what we do lines up with a strong vision that is bigger than just how fast new tech keeps changing. It's like being asked to guide our group or company using a smart map. This will help us in taking the team towards better future where new ideas create impact and last long.

Principle 3. Make first things first

Chapter 1. Introduction to Adaptability in Tech

Principle 3 reminds us to learn how to change. As we embark on this journey, the first chapter unfurls with a fundamental understanding: Learn about Adaptability in Tech. Today, when change happens quickly and deeply, being able to adjust is key for winning. This idea asks us to change how we think. It tells us it's very important to stay flexible and quick when technology is changing all the time.

Being able to change or adjust is not just a talent but it's also a big plan. It's the skill to deal with new and exciting things while also handling changes in technology. This includes moving when it went a different way, imagining good ideas even during tough times. In this section, we create a base by saying that adaptability is an important skill which makes successful tech leaders different.

The Beginning of Flexibility in Technology starts a deep look. It tells us to see that the skill for change is not a quick fix, but something we decide on. We should be strong and ready in an industry where future scenes are based off results gained now.

As we start reading the pages that come after, let this first part stick in our heads - it's like a guide helping us understand how technology changes. It makes us face change not as a problem but something that helps growth. This gives the start for journey where being able to adjust becomes our friend in trying new ways of thinking

In the busy world of technology, where every new thing comes from an earlier one and changes are usual. The ability to change becomes a key part of strategy in this fast-moving area. This start shows not only how important change is, but also the need to put things in order and concentrate on what really matters all the time.

Adapting, in the world of tech leadership is not just a random reaction to change; it's purposeful move where you put what's most important first. It's about seeing through the many choices and technology trends to find what really has true worth. In this always changing world, it's very important to make some things more important than others.

As we deal with the tough parts of technology changing, the start helps us to understand that being flexible isn't about getting swept up everywhere change is happening. It's about making decisions on where our path should go. It asks us to put our efforts on what's really important, understand the signs from all the sounds and make decisions with a clear goal in mind.

Let this beginning sound like a guide for our journey through the future chapters - to remind us that being able to change is not just about responding when something changes, but also making sure what really matters comes first. It gets ready for a trip where starting with the most important things becomes not just an idea but strong rule for winning in tech's always changing land.

Chapter 2. Adaptability and Time Management

Flexibility, as we've shown already, is not a simple way to handle change but rather it's an active and thought-out way of dealing with the changing world caused by tech. In this case, we recognize the close relationship between being able to change and managing our time well.

In the fast-growing world of technology, where changes happen quickly and what is important can change in a second, being good at managing time becomes very important for leaders so they can adjust easily. It's about using time well, knowing that not all jobs or technology changes are the same.

This chapter makes us think about how we spend our most important thing - time. It asks us to accept a changeable way of managing time, knowing that being versatile with what we prioritize is as important as changing along with new technologies. It's about knowing what needs quick action, what can wait and requires a change in how we spend our time.

As we go on this journey, remember that being flexible - when combined with good time keeping - turns us from just reacting to leading change. It's asking us to match our time with the fast pace of technology world. This helps make sure we stay ahead and do it carefully, clear about what should be done first. This part is about getting a big picture view. Time isn't just something holding us back, but it can also help in being an excellent leader for changes and growth in the field of technology when we make good use of it.

In tech leadership, adapting fast and managing time well are connected in a close way. They affect each other like two dancers who have to be careful and quick not to mess up while they move together.

Imagine a situation where someone in charge of computer stuff has to quickly change what they are working on because new trends are happening. They have to do this fast due to changes in the market that surprised them. In this situation, managing time well becomes very important. The boss needs to change deadlines, use resources differently and make sure the team's work matches with changing surroundings. Being able to handle a changing project is all about managing time well. This includes planning tasks, making schedule changes and seeing that important things are dealt with correctly.

Likewise, a leader's flexibility is tested when the arrival of new tech demands changing how their company does business. It needs to shift strategy as well. In these cases, good use of time is important to decide how fast the company can accept and work with a new idea. The boss has to make quick choices, use resources well and direct the team in matching their work with new technology for change. Here, being flexible and managing time well works together. This makes sure that the company not only answers changes but uses them smartly in their plans.

Think about a tech leader managing fast changes in rules and laws. It's important to change for new rules, but the success of that depends on using time well. The boss needs to find time for staying up-to-date with changes in rules, putting them into action if needed and making sure the team has enough knowledge about what's proper.

These examples show the close relationship between being able to change and good time management in tech leadership world that keeps changing. Being able to change relies a lot on how well time is used. Good use of time helps leaders adjust wisely as the company world and technology keep changing constantly. Together, they make a strong team. They help tech bosses not only survive but grow big in the ever-changing world of technology.

As we find the link between this, it's very important to teach tech workers how to choose what matters most and use their time well in a busy technology world.

1. **Clear Goal Alignment**: Tech workers start a trip of smart time use by linking their tasks with big targets. This means carefully checking the goals of an organization and important dates on a project. By building a strong link between individual tasks and the bigger strategic goals, workers can make smart choices about which job is most important. This plan makes sure that we spend our time and hard work on things that help the company do well. It gives meaning to what we do, making every action feel important.

2. **Agile Task Prioritization**: The speed of sorting jobs is a fast way that agrees with the always-changing nature of technology. Tech workers accept that priorities can change, often checking tasks again in response to new needs. This plan needs teams to talk and work together often. They must change as the project needs keep changing. The ability in agile task prioritization lets workers handle uncertainties quickly. This makes sure their energy is focused on the most important and timely actions.

3. **Time Blocking**: Time blocking is a smart plan that goes beyond basic time management. It means setting aside time on purpose for certain jobs or kinds of work. Tech people make a focused space for each job by dividing their workday into different parts. This plan reduces interruptions and doing many things at the same time, helping us focus deeply on what we're working on. Time blocking makes you work better and also helps to make sure important tasks get the focus they need. This leads to more successful results.

Every one of these methods helps tech workers handle the confusing relationship between changing and using time. People work together to help others react and change with the changing tech world. They also plan how they use their time so it matches long-term goals and what's needed for new projects.

Chapter 3. The Agile Mindset

The Agile Mindset, same as being flexible, is not only a way of doing things; it's an idea which helps shape rules that makes us strong and nice to change. Basically, agility in tech leadership means being able to handle uncertainty, welcome change and keep on learning and improving constantly.

A basic idea of the Agile Mindset is making progress step-by-step. Tech bosses are urged to split hard jobs into smaller parts that can be controlled. This lets them check and change things more often. This step-by-step method matches perfectly with the idea of being flexible. It's important to change and adapt plans for them to work out well.

A big idea is focusing on what customers want. The Agile Mindset focuses a lot on learning and fulfilling the changing needs of customers. This idea is linked with how leaders in technology must change along. It's very important to always be ready for the changing needs of customers if they want continued success and importance.

Working together is very important in being agile, it encourages teams with different skills to work closely and always talk. Working together is like being able to change easily. Good talking and teamwork are important in dealing with changes in technology or complicated jobs.

The ability to adapt quickly is a key feature of the agile way of thinking. Instead of strictly sticking to set plans, tech bosses are encouraged to see change as always happening and change their strategies. This flexibility fits well with the need to change in the always-growing world of technology.

Getting into an Agile way of thinking in managing projects helps many ways. It changes how teams solve problems and handle big tasks differently.

1. **Enhanced Flexibility and Adaptability**: The Agile Mindset creates a flexible culture that lets teams quickly adjust to different project needs or unexpected problems. The ability to change keeps project plans flexible and quick, stopping delays and helping with fast problem-solving.

2. **Iterative Progress and Continuous Improvement**: Using the Agile way helps us work in small steps and keep improving. By splitting projects into smaller, easy-to-handle parts, teams can keep checking and improving their work all the time. This going-around process makes teams always better. It lets them learn and adjust their plans in each turn for more successful problem solving.

3. **Customer-Centric Solutions**: The Agile Mindset pays a lot of attention to knowing and serving customer wants. By getting customers involved in making things better and using their

ideas time after time, teams can check that what they make fits real-world needs. This approach that focuses on customers makes projects more successful and important.

4. **Improved Collaboration and Communication**: Working together is a big idea in the Agile way of thinking. Teams that work together from different areas help each other and promote good communication between everyone. This stronger working together makes sure that team members know a lot, agree and can all fix issues when they happen. This leads to a better and stronger way of managing projects.

5. **Reduced Time-to-Market**: The teamwork and step-by-step approach of the Agile Mindset makes projects go faster. By giving small improvements in short time periods, teams can cut down the amount of time it takes to get new products and answers. This fast service not only meets market needs better, but also helps deal with new problems faster.

6. **Risk Mitigation**: The Agile Mindset promotes taking action to manage risk. By dealing with possible dangers over and over again, and frequently checking what is important in the project, teams can find out early on which risks need to be fixed. This early action to manage risk helps in better running of projects and solving problems.

7. **Adaptation to Market Changes**: In fast-moving fields like technology, market situations can change quickly. The Agile Mindset helps teams to handle these changes well. New tools and changes in what people want are all easier to handle for teams working with an Agile process. This way, they can face market challenges well and stay strong.

Choosing an Agile Mindset for project management and problem-solving is a big change that helps teams to handle uncertainty, create new ideas, and give worth faster. The good things go past when a project is done, changing the group's way of working and setting up teams to keep doing well as technology changes all the time.

Let's explore two examples that illustrate the principles of the Agile Mindset in action.

Example 1: Software Development Sprint

In a software project using Agile rules, sprint is a short and limited time (often two weeks) where special features or tasks are made, tested for working properly then sent out. You can see the Agile Mindset in different parts of sprint.

One main idea is constant improvement. The team working on each sprint does part of the features. This lets them keep checking and changing things regularly. At the end of the sprint, a product update ready to ship is delivered. This step-by-step method makes sure that the product changes little by little. It can adapt easily to new needs or opinions from people who matter.

Another rule at work is working together. Developers, testers and product owners work together closely during the sprint in cross-functional teams. Daily meetings help team members talk every day. They share what they've done, talks about problems and make quick choices together. This teamwork makes it easier to solve problems and keeps everyone on the same page with project targets.

The Agile Mindset is also shown in the review at the end of every sprint. People on the team think about what they did good, where they can make it better and how to improve their ways of working. This constant learning and changing makes a mindset of always getting better. It ensures that the team gets more successful with each round they do.

Example 2: Marketing Campaign Launch

In advertising, using an Agile Mindset can change how groups plan and carry out marketing efforts. Let's think about starting a digital marketing campaign for a new product.

Adaptability is shown in the process of making plans. Instead of making a detailed, fixed plan first, the people in charge start with an overall plan and change it as their campaign moves forward. This gives the team a chance to answer back to comments from buyers, shifting ways people behave as customers or surprising chances they didn't expect.

Teamwork is very important. It needs people from marketing, sales and support to work together with others in different areas too. This teamwork between different fields makes sure the campaign fits with general business targets. It also allows teams to quickly tackle new problems or chances that come up.

Giving quick responses is a main idea in Agile marketing. By using stats and opinions from customers, the group can quickly check how well their campaign is doing. They can then use facts to change it if needed. This way makes sure the marketing plan stays in line with what customers need and current market trends.

In both cases, the Agile Mindset means accepting change and working together to keep providing value. In the case of making software or advertising, this way of thinking lets groups deal with unknown things. It also helps them adjust to changing needs and finish tasks quickly in a bustling world.

Chapter 4. Finding Important Goals in Tech Projects

To do well in technology projects, you need to know which tasks are most important and get them done. Our advice is focused on a vital skill. It helps project managers, developers and others see through the challenges of technology projects clearly.

The key part of this plan is to make sure we know exactly what the project will cover. This means making clear goals, tasks and times for a project. It helps find important work that goes with what the project wants to achieve.

To make this process easier, we bring out different sorting ways as helpful tools for good job groupings. Frameworks like MoSCoW (Must-haves, Should-haves, Could-haves, and Won't-haves) and the Eisenhower Matrix teach you ways to choose jobs based on if they are urgent or important. These ways are helpful tools. They help people make thoughtful choices and promote a planned way of deciding which jobs come first.

Teamwork is the main idea, showing how important it is to talk openly and involve key players early on. Working together means that different views help in knowing the big goals and what users need for a project. This shared knowledge helps us decide what is important in a group setting, using our own understanding.

Understanding that technology projects change, flexible ranking becomes very important. Teams are taught to always check and change what is important as a project goes on. This makes sure they can quickly handle new problems, take advantage of good chances, and stay ready for changing customer trends.

The advice given is like a complete tool set. It gives useful information and tactics to help tech teams find important jobs they need to do first. By highlighting the need for a clear goal. we suggest helpful ways to arrange tasks based on importance, support teamwork with those who matter and promote being able to easily change plans when dealing with technology projects.

Let's see two real-life examples where good planning was vital in making successful projects adaptable.

Toyota's change in making things, seen best with the Just-In-Time (JIT) system for production, shows how focusing on what is needed can help adapt to wants from customers. The JIT system focuses on reducing the amount of goods in stock and making just what is needed, exactly when it needs to be made.

In the car business, Toyota was able to quickly adjust to shifts in what people want and market needs due to JIT system. Toyota did not keep big stocks of many car types. Instead, it focused on being able to change its production lines easily. This ability to change allowed them to quickly deal with shifts in what customers liked, new trends that were coming up or sudden changes happening in the market.

During bad economic times or sudden changes in fuel costs, Toyota could change what they make. They might focus more on cars that use less gas or smaller cars to show how flexible their plans can be. This smart way not only made things work better but also put Toyota as the boss in dealing with changing market situations.

In both cases, these groups planned and focused on their tasks well. This helped them handle doubts or changes that came up later. They did it all by being successful in the places where they worked at last. These real-life examples show how being flexible, helped by good planning, is a big part of the success for difficult projects.

In the world of streaming, Netflix has grown into a big player. This is in part because it knows how to prioritize its content well. Netflix's success is not just about making content, it also means choosing the right kind of material that connects with their many fans all over the world.

Netflix uses data-based sorting to find out which types of content like genres, themes and styles should be popular in different areas. The Must-haves are very important TV shows and movies that many people enjoy watching. They help to get more subscribers for streaming services. Things we should have maybe include special types of stories or new ideas, while Things could-have are not as important.

Netflix shows flexibility when it notices that viewers' tastes are changing. For example, if a particular type of story suddenly becomes very popular, they can quickly change their plan. They will focus more on similar ideas in future stories that they make. This change in content focus has been a major reason Netflix stays on top of a business.

Chapter 5. Overcoming Resistance to Change

Beating resistance to change in the tech world can be hard. This is because technology moves really fast. Here are strategies to address common challenges and resistance to change:

1. **In-Depth Communication Strategy**

   Stakeholder Involvement: Get important people, like computer experts, involved in the change process from the start. Run classes, talks and sessions to know their thoughts and worries. Being part of this helps get important ideas and makes people feel like they own something.

   Strategic Messaging: Make a full communication plan that talks about the change in detail. Explain how the change matches with what our group wants to do, where it's going and how technology is changing. Easily tell about the possible good effect for both the company and each team member.

   Two-Way Communication Channels: Create ongoing ways for tech experts to talk back and forth, like special online places or tools. Here they can share their ideas, ask questions and get quick answers in return. Talking openly makes things clearer and cuts down on confusion.

2. **Technology-Centric Upskilling Initiatives**

   Customized Training Programs: Create training programs that focus only on the technology part of change. Make sure these programs include the newest tools, ways of doing things and skills needed for successful change. Make training classes for different skill levels in tech groups.

Hands-On Workshops and Hackathons: Set up workshops and events where technology workers can try out new tech stuff in a safe space. Experiences in real life make you feel sure and excited about the changes, while also encouraging a way of learning that never stops.

Certification Programs: Start certification programs or badges for learning new skills related to the change. Noticing and praising when people get better at their work helps to show the worth of learning new skills. This encourages tech workers to take part in helping themselves learn more.

3. Security and Compliance Assurance

Security Briefings: Hold in-depth talks about safety to deal with worries connected to keeping data safe and private. Clearly show the steps to keep private information safe and follow rules set by different businesses. Talk with online safety experts to explain how strong the security systems are.

Regulatory Compliance Updates: Tell technology teams about any changes in rules that could affect how they put things into place. Keep them informed about how to follow the rules and stress that our company is focused on keeping data safe and private.

Collaboration with Security Experts: Work with outside safety specialists or groups to do separate checks and reviews. Checking by other groups can make security steps more believable and calm worries of tech workers.

4. Agile Implementation Methodology

Incremental Changes: Change things slowly and little by little, repeating the process. Divide the big change plan into smaller parts that are easy to handle. This lets us get small victories fast and shows real improvement, making it simpler for computer groups to adjust.

Frequent Feedback Loops: Set up a system where tech workers can give advice and help during the process of putting in place new technology. Agile ways of working depend on being able to change quickly. Adding feedback helps in making quick changes based on what is happening right now.

Cross-Functional Collaboration: Help tech teams work together with other departments. Teams with different skills can offer many views, promoting a full understanding of the changes. This teamwork method reduces separate groups and encourages everyone to feel responsible for the project's success.

5.   **Cultural Integration of Change**

Align with Core Values: Make sure the suggested changes match with what the organization believes in. Connecting the changes to the basic ideas and goals of the company gives a good reason for getting on board. It encourages a feeling of reason and assists tech workers to link the changes with the bigger goal.

Recognition of Adaptability: Make being able to change a big value in how the company works. Acknowledge and give credit when tech groups show the ability to adapt, be inventive, and tough during change. This understanding supports the change in culture to accept transformation as a good thing.

Storytelling for Culture Building: Use storytelling to share good news about the change. Tell stories about how tech groups beat problems, worked together well and got good results. Telling stories is a strong way to bring cultures together. It helps people feel connected and understand the ideas behind change.

By using these clear plans, companies can handle the difficulties of not wanting change in tech world and promote a culture that likes adapting and new ideas.

Chapter 6. Developing Adaptability Skills

Being good at changing and growing is very important. Here are two practical exercises and tips to enhance adaptability, along with scenarios illustrating successful adaptation.

1.   **Simulation-Based Learning**

Create situations like the real world for tech workers to practice being able to adjust in a safe place.

a. Make pretend situations that show normal problems in the tech world, like fast changes to project plans, new technology updates needed or surprising production troubles.

b. Team Participation: Make teams that have people from different areas and give each team a pretend situation. Tech experts work together to create flexible plans and answers.

c. Debriefing Session: After the practice, have a chat session where groups talk about their methods, problems they faced and things learned. Start talks about other ways to change and adjust.

d. Continuous Improvement Plan: Ask teams to make a plan for always getting better based on what the simulation shows. This plan might need making things better, improving how we talk with each other or learning more in certain topics.

- Stress the need for flexibility and being able to change direction when unexpected problems come up.
- Promote a mindset of wanting to learn and being open for new ideas during the game.
- Show how good talking and working together helps to beat problems.

A tech team has to deal with a fast change in project goals because of changing business needs. The team works well together and makes fast choices. This helps them change quickly, so the project stays on time.

2. Reflective Journaling

Promote understanding of yourself and life-long learning by telling tech workers to think about their experiences often and change how they handle them.

a. Tech experts create a type of diary where they write down daily or weekly work experiences, easy and tough moments. In this journal, they speak about how to overcome these struggles in life.

b. Adaptability Reflections: Make a part of the diary for thoughts on being able to adapt. Tech experts look at cases where they needed to change, finding what worked well and areas needing betterment.

c. Peer Feedback: Start peer review sessions where tech workers can talk about their thoughts with friends. Promote helpful comments and ideas about different ways to adjust.

d. Goal Setting: Using thoughts and comments, tech workers decide on special targets for improving their ability to adapt. These targets might involve going to relevant training events, finding someone to guide you or working on particular methods.

- Show the big deal of knowing yourself to understand your own feelings when change happens.
- Encourage a mindset of improvement, seeing problems as chances to learn and grow.
- Push tech workers to look for different ideas by working with others and getting input.

A tech worker thinks about the feeling of changing to use a new technology with their team. The professional gets feedback and thinks about how to improve. They then work hard on learning new technology since it is important for them.

3. Tech Innovation Challenge

Make tech people think of new ideas and be flexible by asking them to come up with fresh ways to solve a problem using technology.

a. Problem Identifying: Show the team a difficult or unclear tech issue that is related to their field of work. Make sure the challenge needs creativity and flexibility.

b. Cross-Functional Teams: Make teams with people from different jobs and give each team the task of being creative. Promote different skills and views within each team.

c. Solution Prototyping: Teams work together to make new ideas come true. Stress the need for change and ease in making their thoughts better based on responses.

d. Showcase and Evaluation: Groups present their answers to the larger tech group in their company. Help make the assessment process better, showing how it's easy to change and be creative. Also show that something can really work.

- Emphasize the importance of accepting failure as a part of creating new things.
- Promote trying new things and being open to think differently.
- Show how good communication helps in sharing and improving new ideas.

A group of tech people have trouble planning for an advanced project. The team works together to come up with ideas and keep making changes. They handle surprises in technology well, creating a new answer that everyone likes better than they thought it would be.

4. Mentorship Program

Start a program where younger workers teach older tech team members, to help them learn better and be more flexible.

a. Matching Teachers and Learners: Find tech workers who have different amounts of experience. Match skilled experts (mentors) with people who don't have as much experience (mentees), so they can all learn from each other.

b. Skill Exchange Sessions: Hold regular skill swap events where teachers give knowledge about their work and learn new stuff, while students share information on latest technology tools or ways to do things.

c. Adaptive Learning Plans: Work together to create flexible learning plans for both teachers and students. Motivate teachers to learn and change with new technologies taught by students.

d. Feedback and Reflection: Set up regular talks where mentors and learners think about the changes, they learned from being in the reverse teaching program.

- Highlight the importance of learning from different age groups and how it brings varied views.
- Promote talking freely and share ideas without a steep hierarchy.
- Create an environment where everyone, no matter their experience, is viewed as someone who helps the team get better in changing situations.

An experienced builder finds out about a new coding language and build tool from someone younger on his team. The group works together to add this information into their projects. They show that the program of reverse coaching helps growing adaptability.

These extra helpful tricks and activities help tech workers learn different ways to get better at being flexible in many situations inside the tech world.

As we conclude our exploration of Principle 3: In the area of adaptability with changing technology, we look at a place where planning, strength to survive and changes in tools all meet. This idea is like a guiding light. It tells us to focus on being flexible as the main thing for success in technology businesses that change all the time.

We've looked at exciting examples that go beyond theory. They show real-life situations where being able to change has been very important. The story of tech companies changing how they work, moving to the cloud and planning major shifts shows what can be done when you make being flexible an important part of business goals.

The examples in the study show how tech teams, because of changes in technology and market movements as well as new trends. They used clever ways to decide what's really important for them - flexibility! This focus on planning has made project completions faster, increased team happiness and given us a stronger ability to handle the difficult parts of work.

In a simple way, "Put First Things First" helps us to do more than usual when solving problems. It's like thinking in new ways and going beyond old ideas. It makes us see change not as a trouble but as a chance for new ideas and growth. As we learn these things, it helps us lead our teams in new areas of technology change. This will help make ways for success even when there is doubt or unknown problems.

In the future, being able to change and adapt will still be very important. As we move forward to the next part of our journey - working together in "Think Win-Win for teams across different functions" and focusing on being flexible. We bring with us what we have learned before. It becomes the main part we use to create partnership communities. This helps everyone succeed together and reach new heights in always changing tech world. The trip goes on, with a promise to change and create new things in the fun and unknown world of technology.

Principle 4. Think Win-Win in Cross-Functional Collaboration

Chapter 1. Introduction to Cross-Functional Collaboration

Working together between tech and non-tech teams is a key part for overall success. The days of separate operations are over. Now, it's all about being connected and celebrating successes together. When tech experts and people from areas like marketing, finance and others join together without walls between them, teams can work better. This lets everyone grow as part of a bigger success story.

The value of working together is highlighted because real progress frequently happens when different views meet. When computer and non-computer teams work together, many new ideas, skills and experiences are shown. This helps make solutions that not only have good technology but also match bigger business goals better.

In this study, we want to understand the core of working together between many teams. We see it as not only a plan but also a shared belief that is part in everything where groups work with each other. As we go forward, we find the links between tech and not-tech teams. We learn that these areas can be very successful when they work together. "Win-Win Thinking" becomes a main idea. It creates an atmosphere where everyone shares their victories and group success pushes companies higher in the tech world that always changes.

It's very important to highlight the need for a win-win attitude when working together on cross-functional teams. This helps create positive relationships between team members. This way of thinking goes beyond the usual idea of rivalry and instead backs a team effort where one group's success is connected with others.

It's important to focus on a win-win approach when building good teamwork in groups with different roles. This way of thinking goes beyond the normal idea of competition and instead supports a team approach where one department's success is connected to others.

When different teams work together, a win-win approach helps to make the workplace fair and easy going. It makes people from different parts of a company work together. They don't just focus on their own goals, but see them as part of the bigger whole in an organization.

By building this way of thinking, companies can remove the walls that often stop talking and working together.

This idea of working together goes beyond just helping each other; it's about finding ways where everyone involved can benefit. It's about understanding that when tech and non-tech teams combine, they can make results even better than what one individual could do. The idea of win-win thinking makes a situation where the group's success is more important than personal victories.

When we look at the idea of 'Win-Win' in working together across different teams, we explore how taking up this way can change what a company is like. It's about making a mutual goal where each department helps and gains from the total success of the company. By looking at real examples and ideas, we want to show the good results of a helpful mindset. We will not just talk about working together but also how it affects making new things better, solving problems faster and being strong in tech businesses that always change quickly.

Chapter 2. Challenges in Cross-Functional Collaboration

In the complicated group work in technology companies, businesses often have complex problems they need to find their way through. The prevalent challenges that surface in this collaborative landscape are:

1. **Communication Barriers**

   Sometimes, tech and non-tech departments that are linked together can have trouble with how they talk to each other. Using separate ways to talk might cause confusion, wrong understandings and not being clear. If these problems aren't fixed, they can cause bad project results and waste resources.

   A fair-for-both approach helps with communication issues by making honest and clear talking top priority in teamwork. When teams understand that good talking is a common goal with shared benefits, they are more likely to remove communication obstacles. Building a sharing atmosphere makes teams with different skills work together. People feel brave to give ideas, thoughts and opinions which helps communication become clearer between everyone.

2. **Divergent Objectives and Priorities**

The mix of tech and non-tech teams can lead to different goals or focus areas. Not agreeing about big business goals can show up as problems when dividing resources, finishing projects on time and general company aims. Dealing with these differences is a big problem for easy teamwork.

The idea of everyone winning helps bring people together when they have different goals and targets. By getting everybody to agree on what the company wants, tech and non-tech groups can find places where they both work well. This working-together way gets rid of the idea that one person's win means another loses. It makes teams see success as something everyone can have together. It says that when one part of a group does well, it can help the whole organization win. This makes people work together for common goals instead of just their own plans.

3. **Resistance to Change**

Working together across different teams often requires making changes to the usual ways of working. Not liking change can come from tech and not-tech parts, stopping team work projects going smoothly. People might not want to use new ways, machines or group systems.

A positive outlook looks at resistance to change as a chance for everyone's improvement together. By talking about the good things that come from working together, companies can lessen push-back. This method is about getting teams involved in making choices, showing them how changes connect with both personal and group targets. It creates a setting where being flexible is considered as something everyone works on together to achieve joint success.

4. **Lack of Shared Vision**

If there isn't a shared view, working together with different groups may not have a clear goal. Tech and non-tech teams may work separately, each with their own understanding of the company's goals. This misalignment can cause separate attempts, stopping a shared group idea from coming true.

A positive mindset helps develop a common goal that goes beyond group borders. It means setting goals together, making sure that the dreams of both tech and not-tech teams help achieve what our company wants to be. By matching what one person wants with the goals of a group, groups can build teamwork. This strong base lets people from different areas work together better.

5. **Unequal Resource Allocation**

Giving money, time and people to tech and non-tech groups in different ways can upset teamwork. This difference can cause people to be unhappy, think things aren't fair and make team efforts less successful.

A win-win approach says that resources should be shared fairly and equally. This makes sure both tech and non-tech parts get what they need. By making sure that resources are shared fairly, groups can create a team atmosphere where every part feels cared for and important. This method helps to make a good teamwork where all the parts of every group are noticed and valued.

Going into the hard parts of working with different teams, thinking about how everyone can win is a smart guide. It makes companies see problems not as big barriers, but chances to work together and fix them. Tech leaders can team up with others on a win-win basis to work together nicely. This way, they use all kinds of ideas in overcoming problems and create an atmosphere where new things happen quickly. They then help each other become more successful as the world of technology keeps changing every day.

Chapter 3. The Win-Win Mindset in Tech

In the fast-moving world of computers and technology, deciding to help others also helps you is not just about making plans; it becomes a part of your group culture. This affects how companies work together with each other, think up new ideas - and succeed in their jobs.

This way of thinking goes beyond the usual ideas about competition and single wins. In the world of technology, thinking win-

win means recognizing that when tech and not-tech departments work together they can accomplish things better than what just one department could do. It's about making a community where everyone, from software makers to advertising experts sees success as something we do together.

The main idea of working together to win in tech is understanding that the whole team's success will be bigger than just every single person being successful. It's a big change that makes tech people see their work not just by itself, but as important parts of a bigger picture in the company. By promoting this way of thinking, companies make a place where people work together. With the joint force of different groups, they push their whole group to never-before-seen new heights.

Looking at the win-win approach in a tech situation means examining how teamwork is key to successful tech projects. It's about realizing that when tech folks work together with people who aren't in tech, their answers are not just good from a technical standpoint but also match up well with bigger business goals. It's a look at how winning together makes for good workplace culture. It helps to create new ideas, work better and toughness in the company.

In the fast-paced world of technology, choosing to coexist for everyone's benefit is not only a smart move. It becomes a central part of how businesses handle working together, creating new things and achieving success.

This way of thinking goes beyond the usual ideas about competition and winning alone. In the tech world, thinking win-win means understanding that working together between tech and non-tech groups can result in results better than just what one person could do. It's about making an environment where everyone involved, from code writers to sales people. They all see succeeding as something they achieve together.

The meaning of thinking like a winner in tech is to see that the group's accomplishments are bigger than each person doing well. It's a new way of thinking that makes tech workers see their work not just by itself but as important pieces for the big picture in an organization. By helping this way of thinking, companies make a place where teamwork grows. With lots and different groups working together better the whole firm reaches never-seen heights.

Looking at a win-win approach in technology means going into the teamwork feeling that leads to successful tech projects. It's about knowing that when tech workers team up with people who don't work on technology, the solutions they make are not only good for technical reasons but also match bigger business goals. It's a look at how winning together makes good organization vibes, boosting creativity and speed plus allowing us to bounce back stronger.

Using a win-win way of thinking in tech is different than normal win or lose situations. It needs to change how you see things so that success isn't just about winning and losing but everybody working together.

In a usual win-lose situation, it is thought that for one side to come out on top, the other must lose. Often, seeing things in a zero-sum way can make people become rivals. Competition is more important than working together for them. When it comes to the tech world, this thinking could show up as different divisions fighting for things like resources or praise. This can stop everyone from working together and succeeding together properly.

On the other hand, a win-lose situation means that one person willingly gives in or makes compromises for another's advantage. This way, although it seems nice and caring, might cause anger or unfairness inside the group. In the world of tech, this could happen when one part gives up its aims so another can succeed. This might stop new ideas and art from growing strong.

The idea of winning together in tech is very different from these old ways. It shows a way of thinking where success isn't just for one person, but everyone shares it. This is an open approach when the achievements of one part or individual help others win too. The win-win mindset is different from the either you win or I lose way of thinking. Instead, it works best when people work together and help each other to reach big goals.

In technology, this change means knowing that winning a project is not just about being good with tech but also how well it follows overall business goals. This means tearing down walls between tech and non-tech groups, creating a feeling where different teams work easily together instead of fighting for limited things.

The idea of winning together creates an atmosphere where everyone is interested in the group's overall success. It's about taking down the walls that put teams against each other and instead making a teamwork world where different skills and views come together to improve all parts of the organization.

When we explore this idea, it's important to know that thinking in terms of win-win isn't just a smart choice; it's changing the way success is seen and reached by everyone as technology keeps growing.

Chapter 4. Effective Communication in Cross-Functional Teams

Working on teams that include people from different departments needs more than just skill. You've got to know how to talk and understand the differences between tech groups and non-tech ones. Here are two strategies to foster effective communication.

1. **Establish Clear Communication Protocols**

   Set and put into action easy ways to talk that go beyond different parts of a company. Set up a common way of talking and writing to make sure information is passed in an easy-to-understand manner for both techies and non-tech people.

   By making rules for communication, you lessen the odds of confusion and mistakes. This means figuring out ways to talk, deciding how fast answers should come and making sure important details are shared all the time. If it's about project updates, tech requirements or getting opinions, having a usual way helps make sure everyone understands what is happening.

2. **Implement Cross-Functional Workshops**

   Organize team-building workshops with people from tech, marketing and sales departments that involve everyone. These meetings help people understand each other better. They give team members a chance to talk about their jobs, problems and what they expect from the group.

   Workshops with different teams allow for free conversations, removing barriers between departments. Tech experts can talk about technical things in projects, while non-tech groups can give information on what customers need and how the market is doing. This not only makes things easier to understand but also gets people working together because they see the whole picture of how an organization works.

3. **Utilize Interdepartmental Liaisons**

   Assign people from different departments to act as links in communication between technology and non-technology teams. These people, picked from different areas of work, help in sharing information. They make sure that ideas and knowledge are smoothly passed around between teams.

   Liaisons between departments help share information well. They go to meetings, work on projects together and represent their own departments. This plan not only makes talking better, but also creates a feeling of togetherness and shared duty. By making these talk paths, you make sure that important thoughts from non-tech teams are considered in decisions about tech and the other way around.

4. **Establish Unified Project Management Platforms**

   Introduce project management tools that bring together technology and non-technology teams in one online area. These tools should let people work together, share papers in real time. They also help to make departments feel like one big team.

   Common project management tools make it easier to talk by giving all teams a place where they can work together. No matter if it's advertising, making products or helping customers, having one main place makes sure all parts of the company can see what projects are going on. This plan makes talking easier, lessening the chance of wrong understanding and getting different groups working together towards shared aims.

5. **Hold Regular Interdepartmental Forums**

   Set up regular meetings between different departments such as tech, sales and marketing. In these meetups they talk about ongoing projects, problems they have to solve and chances for growth or improvement.

   Meetings between different departments create a structured place for talking. This encourages openness and working together. In these gatherings, people can share news, solve worries and cheer on achievements. It's important to make communication regular, so it keeps happening and doesn't stop suddenly. This plan helps create togetherness, making groups feel like important parts of a big company.

Here are two real-world examples of successful cross-functional projects driven by a win-win mindset

- **Apple's Collaboration with Nike for Apple Watch Nike+**

Apple and Nike worked together to make the Apple Watch Nike+. This product combined tech and fitness in a really smooth way. This joining of forces joined Apple's tech skills with Nike's deep knowledge about fitness and sports markets.

Apple got into Nike's big understanding of how athletes act, tracking health and sports culture. Working together, Apple made the health and fitness features of the Apple Watch better. This made it more attractive to people who like exercise or sports.

Nike used Apple's advanced technology to make the user experience better for its fitness-focused products. The Apple Watch Nike+ is a watch that mixes design, technology and sports smoothly.

The Apple Watch Nike+ did well in the market, liking people who love technology and exercise. This teamwork between different jobs showed how strong it can be to make a product better than what each company could do alone.

IBM and The Weather Company's Data-Driven Decision-Making

IBM bought The Weather Company to add weather information into its cloud and smart computer system. This teamwork focused on making better choices in many fields like farming, moving goods and selling things.

IBM got real-time weather data and forecasting skills from The Weather Company. IBM used this information in its cloud solutions for businesses. This helps them make decisions based on weather forecasts using data.

The Weather Company, now part of IBM, had the chance to grow beyond just giving weather information. It became a very important part of IBM's solutions using data. It provided helpful information that affected many industries beyond weather study.

Working together helped businesses to decide better using weather information. This changed how they managed supplies, used power and other important things in their work. This project showed that mixing knowledge from different areas could result in new answers with wide-spread effects.

These examples show how companies can succeed if they work together in a way that benefits everyone. They use each other's strengths to create things and fix problems that no one could do alone.

By using these big plans, companies can go beyond how they usually work in their parts. This will make a talking system that works well and is all about teamwork and doing good things together. This not only improves understanding between tech and non-tech teams but also sets a base for good talking within all parts inside the business.

Chapter 5. Negotiation and Compromise in Tech Collaborations

Working together on tech projects with different job roles needs a careful knowledge of bargaining methods and why making deals is so important. Working together often needs us to understand different desires, combine views from many sides and keep everyone focused on common goals.

Negotiation in cross-functional tech collaborations involves understanding the intricacies of stakeholder priorities, fostering transparent communication, and focusing on shared objectives.

People who negotiate must look into what different groups want, from tech and non-tech departments. This means truly listening and talking a lot to find out what each person or department wants. The talk starts by finding areas where people agree and match up.

Clear talking is very important for good negotiations to succeed. Setting up ways for people involved to voice worries, hopes and limits helps create trust. Trust then becomes the perfect place for agreement to grow, as partners are more ready to look at a fair point when they feel listened too and understood.

It's important to change the way we talk in negotiations from just my own interests, to goals that everyone wants. Finding big goals that fit with the common mission of working together makes a uniting thread. In this case, making a deal helps to settle different ways and ideas. It guides the teamwork towards one common goal.

Unexpected problems or chances show up. A flexible negotiation style that adjusts to changing situations is important. In this situation, make deals isn't just a single thing. It happens all the time to keep projects with many people strong and able to change when needed.

Finding the right mix between great technology and what users want is a difficult. Understanding that tech teams and non-tech groups might have different goals, making a deal means discovering ways to improve both technical details and user happiness. It makes sure the end result is top in both technical skills and experiences.

In the context of teamwork for technology, giving up in a way that helps everyone is an action you plan and think about rather than just one little change. Here's deeper exploration of the significance and nuances of compromise in fostering successful collaborations:

- **Strategic Compromises**: Compromises are important choices made to match the different plans and goals of tech teams and non-tech ones. They mean looking for shared ideas that help the big goals of working together on a project. This match-up makes sure that each step helps a lot in making the whole project successful.
- **Synergistic Compromises**: Sacrifices are not just about finding a balance; they are about making good combinations. Successful deals make results better than adding up all the parts. By mixing know-how with people's needs, or agreeing on different wants, changes become chances for new ideas and better results in projects.
- **Cultural Compromises**: Compromises help create a teamwork environment in mixed-role teams. They help create a setting where people on the team appreciate knowing and respecting different viewpoints. This teamwork culture becomes the main reason for good talking, trust and a united promise to beat problems together.
- **Adaptive Compromises**: In the always changing world of technology, trade-offs are not fixed; they change with time. Teams have to be ready to go back and change compromises because of changing conditions. This ability makes sure the team project stays strong and ready for new chances or difficulties.
- **Conflict-Resolving Compromises**: Deals are very important for fixing fights that can happen between people who work with technology and those who don't. They give a helpful way to deal with arguments and find solutions that are good for everyone.

When we think of solving problems, disagreements can change into chances for growth by making compromises.

- **Satisfying Compromises**: Deals aren't only about finding a halfway point; they are about pleasing the needs and wishes of people from various groups. Good deals make both sides happy because everyone's needs are considered and used in the work done together.
- **Continuous Improvement Through Compromises**: Making changes helps us get better step by step. As teams work together and learn from each other, the choices they make in one part of a project help to guide choice-making later on. This step-by-step method makes sure that adjustments help improve the project continuously.

In simple words, compromise is a changing and planned activity that turns possible fights into chances for new ideas, working together and mutual success. It needs to think of compromise not as a negative thing, but more like using different talents and ideas from everyone on the team. This will help their joint project progress better.

Giving in a bit, or compromise, isn't weak. It helps groups find their way through hard stuff and join different views together. It helps create a sense of togetherness, strength and flexibility in working with different groups. Successful teamwork in the fast-changing world of tech needs skill to agree and find middle ground. This helps projects reach their goals together, winning all round.

These examples of successful talks give important clues on making good deals that are fair for both sides. Here are two notable examples:

Microsoft and Novell

In 2006, two big companies in the software world - Microsoft & Novell had an important discussion. They aimed to fix problems between their operating systems: Windows by Microsoft and SUSE Linux by Novell. Microsoft saw that Linux was becoming more popular in big businesses and the need for open-source solutions was growing. In the talk, both businesses recognized they had different opinions in software market but cleverly found a place to agree for their customers.

The businesses made a big, new deal to work together on patent problems. Microsoft promised not to sue small, non-commercial open-source developers using SUSE Linux. This helped create a place where everyone respected and worked together nicely.

The talks were about making Windows and SUSE Linux work better together. Both sides agreed to create and share technologies that let their systems work smoothly together. This helps users of the technology and makes it easier for different platforms to connect with each other.

Google and Apple

In 2018, Google and Apple talked about teaming up again over using Google search as the main option on browsers by Apple. They are in a smartphone race against each other. Even though they are big rivals in the smartphone market, both companies knew their teamwork was important. The talk tried to get a deal that would be good for both sides, making money and giving user helpful experience.

The talk led to a deal where Google agreed to pay Apple lots of money. This kept them the main search choice on Safari browser. This setup helped Apple make money while making sure Google stayed in charge of the search engine market.

Both companies knew how important it was to give people an easy and enjoyable experience. The talk included talks about how to make Google's search better inside Apple system. This helps improve the experience for people who use Apple devices.

These examples show how good bargaining works, where important give-and-take and smart agreements resulted in results that were best for all people involved. They show how important it is to find things that both sides agree on, talk about specific problems and use each other's strengths. This helps make a situation good for everyone involved.

Chapter 6. Developing a Collaborative Culture

Making an organization's team work together is not just a target, but very important for long-lasting success. Bosses are very important in making and supporting this cooperative spirit, they make a place where people grow well together. Here's an exploration of how leaders can cultivate and nurture a collaborative culture:

1. **Leading by Example**: Leaders help create a teamwork culture by actively joining in and highlighting the value of working together. They don't just talk about teamwork; they show it in their actions and conversations. Leaders show how important teamwork is by joining together with their coworkers on tasks or having open talks. This practical way not only makes trust but also sets rules for the whole company. It helps create a place where teamwork isn't just wanted by people, it is needed too.

2. **Establishing Clear Communication Channels**: A key part of working together well is clear and honest talking. Leaders are very important in making a place where people feel at ease to give their thoughts, state worries and join conversations. They make sure there are good ways to talk and pass on information inside the company. This means not just telling others about news and choices, but also asking for comments or suggestions from the group. Leaders make sure everyone is informed and feels important by promoting a setting where anyone can talk openly. This way, decisions are better understood by all people involved in them.

3. **Encouraging Cross-Functional Collaboration**: Leaders understand that real teamwork goes beyond individual groups or sections. They strongly promote and help teamwork between different jobs, removing walls that might stop the sharing of ideas and skills. When bosses make chances for groups from different parts of the business to work as a team, they help everyone understand bigger goals better. This way of working together improves solving problems. It also helps in a better, more connected method to reach common goals. Leaders are like spark-starters. They create a place where working together becomes normal and expected in an organization's culture.

4. **Recognizing and Celebrating Team Achievements**: Bosses know that promoting togetherness and common success inside the company is very important. They pay attention and praise their team's accomplishments, stressing that winning is a group job. When leaders praise the efforts of people and groups, it gives them a feeling of happiness and makes them want to do more. This understanding helps to make a strong support for working together. It shows that everyone's work makes the whole group or company better. Leaders make people work together better and stay loyal by celebrating often. This makes everyone feel good about teamwork.

5. **Nurturing a Culture of Inclusivity**: In a real team-based culture, bosses work hard to support inclusiveness. They see the power that can be found from different viewpoints and they ask for advice or ideas from people with varied backgrounds, experiences and skills. When leaders value different opinions, they make a place where everyone feels listened to and important. This way of including everyone not only makes the decision-making better but also helps to create a work place where people feel like they belong. Leaders strongly support difference and inclusion as important parts of the teamwork culture they want to grow.

In short, leaders have many parts to play in making a team work together. They show they value what the group achieves and give them tools for better cooperation while also encouraging everyone to be included. These actions, when done carefully and often makes a workplace where teamwork is not just liked but its core in what everybody believes in. It's how the whole group works too.

Chapter 7. Interactive Workshops on Cross-Functional Collaboration

Interactive Workshop 1: "Collaboration Simulation"

In this hands-on class, people pretend to be part of different teams in a made-up company. Each group has their own job with specific aims and problems they need to solve. The game shows a situation where these offices need to work together to solve the same organization problem. The details of the game are made to look like real-world teamwork where different groups work together.

1. Role Assignment: People are given jobs like advertising, money handling and running. Every job has different goals and limits, making clear the variety of views in teamwork between two or more departments.
2. Challenge Introduction: A usual problem, showing true workplace obstacles, is given. It might be a change in the market, problem with use of resources or moving to better technology. The problem is made to need teamwork for a successful answer.

3. Collaboration and Decision-Making: People talk, work out deals and make choices to solve the problem. Helpers give advice to make sure that people understand the needs of other departments. They help them find solutions where both sides win together.
4. Debriefing: When the simulation ends, a discussion time is given. During this talk, people can think about what they did and how it helped or stopped them from reaching their goals. Helpers lead talks to get main lessons, focusing on using win-win ideas in a team situation.

Interactive Workshop 2: "Case Study Analysis"

This workshop dives into real-life examples of successful teamwork between different roles. It lets people look at and understand the actions happening in those situations.

1. Case Study Selection: Different industries and companies show examples in their case studies. Every case study shows a special problem, the teamwork methods used and the good results made.
2. Group Analysis: People are put into teams to look at certain examples closely. They talk about the problems these groups face, use ideas that are good for all sides and how it affects their overall success. This helps people work together to solve problems in the workshop area.
3. Application to Real Scenarios: Then, groups use what they learned from the examples to solve their own cross-team problems. This part encourages hands-on knowledge about applying win-win ideas in the workplace of all attendees.
4. Sharing Insights: Every group shares their results, encouraging a lively exchange of thoughts. Leaders help guide talks so everyone can fully discuss how to use win-win strategies in teamwork across roles.

Interactive Workshop 3: "Cross-Functional Communication Lab"

This class is about making speech better between mixed groups, a very important part of building a good-for-all mindset. The class-like session includes hands-on activities designed to make people better at talking with others in different parts of a company.

1. Communication Styles Exploration: People join in activities that show different ways of talking found often on mixed work groups. This might use tests on personality or active situations to see and know different ways of talking that people prefer.
2. Role-Playing Scenarios: By acting out situations, people practice how to communicate with others in real life. These situations might be about sharing important details, fixing disagreements or agreeing on what we want to do in a project. Helpful people give advice to make talking better.
3. Feedback and Reflection: After every pretend-play situation, people get helpful advice from others and leaders. This circle keeps giving help for constant improvement. It lets people get better at talking to others with real-world information right away.
4. Developing a Communication Toolkit: At the end of a class, everyone works together to make tools for talking. This toolkit has tips, tricks and successful methods for promoting open and good communication in teams with different jobs.

Interactive Workshop 4: "Strategic Alignment Game"

This workshop for planning brings together different parts of a business, focusing on the need to work toward common goals and make decisions together.

1. Goal Definition: People in a group together make plans for an imaginary company. These goals use ideas from different groups, making sure they are all linked together and have a mix of views.
2. Resource Allocation Simulation: The workshop starts a game about sharing resources. Players have to work together, giving out things needed for different projects based on what they want to get done. This activity promotes talks about what's important, choices one has to make and finding solutions that are good for all sides.
3. Decision-Making Challenges: Helpers put decision-making tasks, showing that working together from different groups is always changing. People deal with these problems, using fair and helpful ideas to make things better for the whole company.
4. Reflection and Action Planning: The workshop ends with a think-about session where people talk about what they learned. Every person makes a plan that shows how they will

blend good-for-all ideas into their team plans. This helps them work better together with other teams for improved cooperation.

These classes help people better understand working together with different groups by emphasizing how to talk well and match strategies. By doing real activities, people not only understand the theory but also get practical skills they can use right away to make their teams work better together in their jobs.

During those workshops, people are also asked to think about how they work together now and decide on goals for improvement.

1. **Self-Reflection Exercises**: People take part in self-reflection activities that make them think about how well they work together. They look at what's good and find ways to get better. This part makes people think about themselves and learn how they work together with others.

2. **Peer Feedback and Support**: People are told to ask their friends what they think about working together. This back-and-forth sharing helps to create a helpful atmosphere where people can learn from each other's experiences and views. Help from friends is very important in getting better all the time.

3. **Personalized Action Plans**: People make plans for themselves by looking at their own actions, setting goals and getting advice from friends. These plans list clear steps, ideas and timeframes for reaching their teamwork goals. The focus is on making reachable goals for steady improvement.

4. **Check-In Sessions**: People meet regularly to talk about their progress, problems and get extra help if necessary. These meetings give a clear plan for responsibility and help people feel like they're all working together to grow in teamwork skills.

By using self-reflection and setting goals in team learning, people not only learn about their own ways of working together. They also take charge of personal growth journey by doing so. This way helps people to really try harder and get better at working together. It makes teams with different jobs stronger, helping the whole company reach its goals.

In conclusion, thinking in a win-win way for teamwork is not only good planning; it's changing how we think about working together on teams and with different departments. By stressing the importance of good results for everyone, groups can make a place where working together is not only allowed but pushes forward new ideas and speed up things. This leads to success all around in general.

This idea shows how important it is to get benefits from each other when facing problems and reaching common aims together. The workshops, examples and activities shown in this idea help people get real-life advice and methods to use a win-win way. This helps them work better on teams with different jobs each day.

When we work in today's big offices, where all groups have to get along. We need a mindset that makes everyone happy and turns them into strong teams who can perform really well together. The path to teamwork across departments isn't just about quick wins; it is about creating a way of thinking where each group member, no matter their job or part of the company does not only play a role but helps make the whole business successful.

As we take this idea to heart, let's remember that working together is not a game with only one winner but instead offers chances for all of those involved to do well. By thinking about winning together, we make a path for the future. This leads to teamwork that includes new ideas and changes easily while everyone works hard towards doing their best work well.

Principle 5. Seek First to Understand, Then to Be Understood

Chapter 1. Introduction to Effective Problem-Solving in Tech

Effective problem-solving is, in fact, the pulse of technology – the heartbeat that resonates with innovation and progress. In a world where hurdles always accompany me around and resolve often change like chameleon, the capacity to solve complex issues is not just an advantage; it is survival. Principle 5 sums up the phrase try to understand, then be understood; reveals that deep insights into problems lead to in-depth solutions.

There are a lot of complication which requires excellent problem-solving abilities. This principle creates the environment because it stresses that knowing is more important than trying to know. it recognizes that deep understanding of the problem landscape is a foundation upon which effective and sustainable solutions in dynamic tech environment lies.

This principle highlights active listening and empathy as key aspects of successful problem-solving. It transcends superficial understanding, encouraging people to dig deeper and understand the underlying worries, interests, factors that influence what should be done about tech-related issues. In a world where complex problem often overlap, the capacity to understand positions of stakeholders serves as an accelerator for meaningful and effective solution-building.

The potency of this principle is illustrated with real-world case studies. These stories are shedding lights, presenting situations where broad knowledge of a problem's complexities led to breakthrough solutions. These examples provide understanding to people how seek-first-to understand approach is used for addressing tech challenges in various aspects of life.

It carries the principle further to eliminate communication barriers that can hamper understanding in technical problem-solving situations. Communication gaps are identified and addressed so that there is room for understanding. This proactive approach to communication issues guarantees that the information flow necessary for effective problem solving remains unimpeded.

Principle 5 beyond interpersonal skills acknowledges the need to develop analytical and critical thinking abilities. These are the tools that equip individuals to deconstruct tech problems systematically. The principle empowers individuals with cognitive power by offering strategies towards development which enables them to solve intricacies and come up with sound solutions.

The principle recommends the use of problem-solving workshops where theory and practice converge. These immersive activities involve collaborative participation in simulated tech problems. Hands on such workshops serve to not only perfect problem-solving skills but also deepens their engraving of the seek first to understand philosophy as they are dealing with challenges at real time.

Essentially, Principle 5 is a testament to the power of understanding in problem solving. It resonates with the sentiment that solutions crafted as a result of profound understanding are also stronger and contribute to perpetual evolution in any given tech industry. It calls upon people to adopt the principle as a guiding spirit through which one can traverse all periods of change in dealings with technological challenges.

The nature of this principle comes out in the very basic idea that our understanding should come before trying to convey one's own point. It calls the notion that in every interaction or problem-solving attempt, one should first concentrate on understanding perspectives concerns and intricacies presented by others.

Through the principle of first understanding and then speaking, it encourages a transformation in attitude – one that makes genuine understanding central to interpersonal relations. This principle encourages people not to rush into the impulse of stating their views but rather taking time and effort in understanding the whole picture of information that has been presented.

The underlying philosophy resonates with the idea that exclusive solutions and effective cooperation arise from a deep comprehension of circumstances, difficulties, and perspectives. It acknowledges the complementarity of problem-solving and communication by saying that in order to develop genuine connections, knowledge is important for making informed decisions.

This principle can be considered a guiding star for building an environment where active listening, empathy and open-mindedness are applied. It highlights the transformative nature of relating to interactions with an earnest curiosity in order to understand others' points. This introduction of such a principle sets people unto conversations and common works with minds oriented to exploration and comprehension, which implies the preparation for deep problem-solving and interpersonal relationships enrichment.

Chapter 2. Emotional Intelligence and the Power of Empathetic Problem-Solving

Empathetic problem-solving has been a source of light in the manor of successful and transformative resolutions. This part discusses the deep effects of empathy on problem-solving, relating it to a powerful force that transcends more than just technical skills.

In the tech-related challenges, where systemic complications often come hand in hand with human factors, empathy emerges as a beacon on their path. Quite simply, it is no mere soft skill; rather an intelligent instrument that can help people engage with the human parts interwoven in every issue. Empathetic problem-solving goes beyond the surface by recognizing and understanding the emotions, motivations, and limitations of those involved.

This section of the principle indicates that empathy is not simply an observer but a participant in other people's experiences. It means stepping into the shoes of stakeholders, users or even team members to understand their problems. This is the catalyst that creates solutions technically sound and human.

The conversation evolves to demonstrate how empathy becomes the link between technological complexities and human existence. It creates a co-operative atmosphere where individuals feel heard, appreciated and understood. This in turn provides a fertile ground for more open communication, idea exchange and innovative problem solving.

Emotional problem-solving is particularly important in technical scenarios where end-users are the frontliners. This makes it integrally important to understand their needs, frustration and aspirations so that solutions can be crafted that they will resonate with. By recognizing the strength of empathy, users can find their way through this complex equilibrium between technological necessities and people experiences resulting in solutions that are efficient but still user-centered.

Essentially, this portion of the principle celebrates how empathy can change one for good during a process of solving problems. It questions the idea that technical expertise is enough in an increasingly changing arena of technology. By gaining and developing empathy, people open the door to solutions that do not only address the technical details but also connect with human aspects in every challenge.

Let's get into some tech successes where users and stakeholders understanding was the star in problem-resolution.

Imagine a website for online shopping where it appears to know your preferences even better than you do. This is not magic; it's the outcome of a tech team deeply interpreting user behavior. They came up with an individualized shopping experience by looking into past purchases, wish list items as well as browsing habits of the users. The result? Users felt understood, which adopted to a better engagement hence satisfaction and of course more successful transactions.

In the health technology sphere, a group of individuals aimed at developing a mobile application that tracks and facilitates management of chronic disorders. The key to their success? Considering the range of users - from young, tech-savvy millennials to aging individuals with varying degrees of digital literacy. More than just monitoring health metrics, the app turned out to be a user-friendly friend providing customized insights and support. Understanding of this resulted in healthier outcomes and a more diverse technology solution.

The teams that studied the subtleties of individual learning styles are operating in the sphere of edtech. They made education completely tailored by incorporating adaptive learning algorithms and personalized recommendations. Students received content related to their strengths and shortcomings, teachers obtained insights into personal development progresses, the overall educational process became more effective and aimed at customers.

These cases show how addressing and understanding users, stakeholders lead to a transformation in the process of solving technical problems. But it is not simply about the functionalities of that technology; to be truly effective, those solutions need to chime with the genuine needs and preferences - as well as obstacles being faced by people using them. These successes are a sign of the fact that when

tech teams prioritize user understanding then they open to innovations
and positive impacts.

Chapter 3. Active Listening

This segment discusses the idea of active listening as a
transforming phenomenon within the tech environment. Effective
listening is not just about hearing words, it's more like tuning into the
rhythm in between lines, catching those subtle details that define ideas
and innovations. In the world of technology where collaboration
continues to be an essential facet, active listening becomes that special
ingredient which turns a mundane information exchange into musical
understanding.

The exploration starts with uncovering the depths of active
listening – going beyond just hearing and acknowledging the words
spoken. It involves uncovering the hidden motivations, fears and hopes
embedded in every tech talk. Active listening becomes the linking
mechanism that connects seemingly unrelated points of view and forms
a harmonious story, which empowers collaborative initiatives.

This principle states that active listening is not an inactive
practice; it involves a conscious effort of engaging another person's
thoughts and insights. Active listening becomes the catalyst in the tech
tapestry, allowing for capturing collective intelligence of a team and
leading projects forward on an aligned vision.

More than mere person-to-person interaction, active listening
in tech is just as important during project meetings, brainstorming
sessions and code reviews. It's about establishing a space where every
voice is not only listened to but also respected – the kind of atmosphere
in which ideas can crash into one another, blend with each other and
grow together to form something that has meaning far beyond what any
single member would be able to achieve for herself.

In the grand narrative of tech, where message is code and
people are numbers-active listening becomes the hero, we forgot. It's
the unseen force that makes sure that each keystroke, every line of
coding and even ideas is aligned to contribute in sync with symphony of
tech progress.

First, one will need to understand the meaning of active listening but then also incorporate various techniques below that are used when implementing this skill. Here are two techniques and accompanying exercises to enhance active listening skills in the tech arena.

1. **Pair Programming Reflection**: Pair programming in the technology world refers to two developers working together on one code. For instance, take a session where one person is the driver - he or she writes code while another person; The navigator reads and offers insights. Interchange roles after a coding interval. But first, the navigator needs to practice reflective listening before switching. They outline what they understood from the code, ask questions about concerns or suggestions and seek to clarify anything. This not only improves collaborative coding but also hones active listening skills.

2. **Stand-up Meditation:** In the dynamic environment of daily meetings, incorporate an element of mindful silence. Each team member shares their updates and then there is a short break for everyone to think about what was said. Ask team members to note down important points from their colleagues' updates. After silence, go around the virtual or physical room and let each person state their reflections. This exercise promotes listening not just but also the retention and comprehension of information that is passed on.

3. **Code Review Paraphrase:** In the art of code reviews, effective listening is demonstrated through phenomenal paraphrasing. Once team member should talk to another and present their code while the other listens actively. The listener then paraphrases what they believe they have understood regarding the code - explain logic, functionalities and possible improvements. The paraphrase is validated by the presenter, and any discrepancies become objects of discussion. This practice not only enhances active listening but also fosters a deep comprehension of the codebase.

4. **Tech Q&A Jam**: organize a Tech Q&A Jam session where team members in turn ask and answer some tech-related questions. The catch? The individual posing the question has to listen actively and ask a probe question. This questioning does not only enhance active listening skills, but it also fosters deeper engagements in tech topics.

By adding these techniques and exercises to tech-focused activities, individuals can develop a culture of active listening. These practices are more than just recognizing information; they foster a deeper comprehension, facilitates free communication and support synergy that is vital to successful programs of technology.

Chapter 4. Understanding Stakeholder Needs

We start by unfolding the stakeholder layers – those with a vested interest in making sure their tech project is successful. As we transition from end-users seeking effortless experiences to investors looking at the prospective return on investment, every stakeholder has their own set of needs and expectations as they get onto that tech stage.

The tech landscape is, in fact, one colossal act where the audience or stakeholders are truly powerful enough to help write the plot. That understanding becomes the compass that guides the development team through all intricate plot twists of project requirements, budget restrictions and timeline expectations.

Such a principle means that understanding the art of stakeholder needs is not one time action but an evolving dialogue as long as the project lives on. It includes interpreting silent wishes, pre-empting possible obstacles and aligning tech projects with overall objectives of the stakeholders.

In the big picture of technology, stakeholders are not mere spectators; rather they being a part in shaping events. Knowing what users want tech teams can adapt their performances and make sure that every bit of code or feature introduced impacts the intended audience.

The importance of understanding stakeholder needs in tech is not only limited to project development but also influences user experience design, product innovation and long-term sustainability. It concerns the development of tech solutions that not only fulfil functional needs but also resonate with those invested in the success of a given project.

With every step we take in tech projects, let's not overlook those who can be orchestra conductors to strike a chord between different stakeholders and birth success into an entire echo chamber that is our technology ecosystem.

Continuing with the real-world examples, we are able to see how understanding stakeholders contributes to making tech products successful and impactful in society. By addressing the interests and desires of different stakeholder groups, companies have not only become market leaders but also helped address broader societal purposes and goals.

Amazon's Customer-Centric Approach

Amazon's success as a leading e-commerce company is based on the fact that it fully understands its main stakeholder – the customer. From the time Jeff Bezos founded Amazon, customer satisfaction was given priority. Amazon continued evolving to the customer's expectations through data analytics, personalized recommendations and unflagging attention towards convenience. The company's ability to anticipate and meet the changing demands of its varied clientele has made it one of the most reputable stakeholder-centric innovators.

Microsoft's Inclusive Design in Technology

Microsoft's commitment to inclusive design shows that it knows how varied people are in their needs including disability users. They have included features such as Narrator, which is a screen-reading tool and various accessibility options in their products. This approach does not only attract a wide audience but also demonstrates an understanding of the varied stakeholder environment, recognizing that technology should reach everyone. Microsoft's inclusive design philosophy has helped improve its products as well create a standard for tech environments that care about the needs of all users.

Airbnb – A Community-centric Model

Airbnb was a disruptor in the hospitality sector as it reinvented traveler and host relationships. By bridging the gap between travelers seeking unique and personalized accommodations, as well as hosts looking to make money off of their space, Airbnb crafted a platform based on community. It is the advantage of such a company to be able to find the balance between interests of stakeholders - to ensure that hosts can earn money within its platform and at the same time, travelers have possibility to get more authentic as well as individualized accommodations. Airbnb's model incorporates a subtle grasp of the diverse demands present within its stakeholder ecosystem.

Zoom as Fast Responder to Remote Work Needs

With the world moving into remote work, it was on November Zoom Virtual Fashion Show held its that deal with fashion and culture stood out. As virtual communication needs soared, Zoom quickly evolved the platform for delivering stable and convenient video conferencing options. Zoom addressed one of the key needs in the stakeholder landscape by understanding that remote collaboration is urgent and problematic. The success also pointed towards the need of responsive technology in times drastic change when keeping business running was more important.

These illustrations emphasize how companies that carefully understand the various needs and tastes of their stakeholders not only manage to survive but thrive in volatile and competitive markets. Companies that make a lasting impact are those able to adapt and innovate based on understanding the stakeholders just like tech companies.

Chapter 5. Effective Communication in Problem-Solving

This segment explores the techniques that transform communication from pure dialogue to a harmony of clarity where every note sounds with precision.

1. **The Art of Simplification**: Problems often appear to be wrapped in layers of intricacy. Simplification is the first rule of the art of effective communication during problem solving. Make complex technical jargon and intricate concepts easy to swallow. A good translator takes a foreign language and converts it into one's mother tongue, just as effective communicators take complex problems and makes them easier to understand by everyone. Suppose a software bug that puzzles even the developers and non-tech participants. Rather than getting into the details of programming, good communication simplifies things by using analogies or metaphors that relate to both individuals so there is a common understanding about what may be going wrong.

2. **Visual Storytelling**: Although words are mighty, sometimes they need to be accompanied by visuals in order to tell the full story. The second approach involves the use of visual

narration. Use diagrams charts and infographics to highlight the problem as well as possible solutions. Just as an architect employs blueprints to share a vision, tech professionals can utilize visuals in order to guide stakeholders through the details of problem-solving process.

A picture of the current state and proposed architecture for a system integration issue can serve as an actual map. This means that stakeholders can better understand the technical details through a visual story, thus promoting comprehension and engagement.

3. **Stakeholder-Centric Communication**: Stakeholders play an important role in problem solving. The third strategy concerns stakeholder-centric communication. Adapt your communication approach to reflect the particular demands and knowledge of your audience. Use the development language while talking to tech teams, switch over to a more strategic conversation with non-tech stakeholders and create an interactive dialogue that bridges both camps.

    During the problem-solving meeting, a tech lead may focus on technical details with his teams of developers by using language that only those in the industry would understand. However, in another session with executives or non-tech team members the conversation changes to address the larger picture and strategic consequences without getting too technical.

4. **Iterative Feedback Loops**: Communication is not one way, it's an interactive exchange. The fourth strategy pertains to building feedback loops. Promote open dialogue and active involvement inviting stakeholders to provide their viewpoint, ask questions or just discuss the topic. So, the two-way communication creates a collaborative atmosphere where ideas can be improved and solutions created together.

    Hold regular feedback sessions during the problem-solving process. This can be achieved through virtual meetings, collaborative platforms or feedback forms built to allow stakeholders' contribution of information so that the evolving problem and their potential solution are understood better.

5. **Storytelling for Impact**: There is a story behind every technical challenge. The fifth strategy involves story-telling as a vehicle for impact. Create a captivating storyline about the problem and its solution. Humanize the technical aspects by demonstrating real-world effects and how effective problem solving can

deliver positive outcomes. Converting data into a story enables stakeholders empathically.

The story telling when talking of a data security breach can be centered around the loss that it might make on users' privacy and what was done to strengthen the system. Communication through crafting a resonating narrative on values and concerns of stakeholders becomes an effective tool in mobilizing support for the initiatives towards problem solving.

In the masterpiece of tech problem-solving, effective communication proves to be the star that brings together different views and leads stakeholders through so many moves in finding a solution. By adopting these strategies and adding clarity and resonance to the problem-solving narrative, tech professionals can make communication not just an exchange of words but a symphony that vibrates throughout every voice in stakeholder choir.

A smart communicator is keenly aware of potential pitfalls that may hinder progress in solving a problem. With that in mind, we focus here on the most frequently encountered communication bumps and suggest ways to avoid them with grace while navigating what can be a tricky road through technological obstacles.

1. **Assumption Alley**: One common trap on the road to good communication is assuming that audience comprehension. Tech professionals, who are well versed in the complexities of their trade may sub consciously assume that everyone knows as much about them as they do. Such an assumption might lead to misunderstandings, confusion and a breakdown in communication.

    Active clarification is the key to avoiding Assumption Alley. Instead of assuming a common understanding, tech professionals should actively test the audience's familiarity with technical terms, concepts and processes. Encourage stakeholders to ask questions, seek clarification and voice concerns. Being open to a questioning mindset creates an atmosphere where communication is reciprocal, so misguided assumptions don't undermine the conversation.

2. **Jargon Junction**: The lure of semi-geeky language is definitely a communication pitfall, especially when interacting with nontechnical stakeholders. In order to include jargon, industry-specific terms should not be used without the proper context

because it can lead to confusion and alienation. Jargon can be a barrier to language, which may inhibit effective communication and hinder the cooperation of teams with technology and those without it.

Using plain language strategically means avoiding Jargon Junction. Tech professionals must consciously strive to translate the technical jargon into easy-to-understand language. Analogies and metaphors can serve as significant devices to present technical ideas in a comprehensible way. Before diving into technical debates, clarify the stage by giving a short introduction and background to the terms that would be used. Communication becomes inclusive and accessible by focusing on the clarity of communication as opposed to being overly technical.

3. **Silence Snare**: This communication pitfall appears when there is no proactive way of communicating and hence various assumptions are made, misunderstanding ensues. This potential pitfall often surfaces when people are unwilling to share their thoughts, concerns or questions. The lack of clear communication can leave open a gap essentially filled with assumptions that may have the potential to derail projects or cause delays.

    To avoid the Silence Snare, establish a culture of open discussion among tech teams. Invite team members to speak their minds, ask questions and provide insights. Establish frequent check-ins that could be either formal or informal so as to give team members a chance of voicing their opinion. Understand the importance of transparent communication as a way to prevent misunderstandings and create an environment in which ideas can be shared openly.

4. **Email Avalanche**: A common challenge in tech communication is Drowning Over relying on email especially for consideration that requires a more complicated discussion or urgent issues has the tendency to distortion of meaning, overlooked messages and an overloaded communication situation. It might also become difficult to collaborate efficiently when important details get buried in lengthy email threads.

    Escape the Email Avalanche by implementing varied channels of communication depending on what is said or discussed. Use project management tools, collaboration platforms or specific communication channels for certain subjects. Use emails only

shared ownership culture on problems, creativity and efficiency. As the team becomes more synchronized and reinforced, these practical tools and frameworks unite to form an active arsenal that empowers teams to overcome problems collaboratively drawing on each other's skills in generating creative results.

Chapter 7. Overcoming Technical Challenges

The discipline of problem-solving is unavoidable in the technology where invention flows through every blood vessel and obstacles are inevitable. To be able to cope with these challenges, one should take a balanced and multi-faceted approach combining technical knowledge with strategic reasoning. Let us take a dive into the world of typical technical issues and discover means to get around them, so that our journey towards effective problem-solving remains bright.

1. **Harmonizing Legacy Systems**: Legacy systems, which are often considered to be prestigious developments in the history of something, can become obstacles for straightforward resolving issues because they use outdated architects. An in-depth system audit is critical to harmonize this technological cacophony. This process involves understanding the complexities of legacy infrastructure components, identifying fundamental dependencies and evaluating migration feasibility. A gradual system modernization becomes a strategic move. Instead of a complete overhaul, gradual advances and modular architecture integration make for an easier transition. 4 This strategy avoids disruptions as the legacy system naturally adapts to the requirements of current solutions. Through meticulous planning of this transition, tech teams will be able to reframe what would have appeared as a dissonant chord into the perfect consonance between heritage and innovation.

2. **Interweaving Technologies**: The pursuit of interoperability, as seen in today's tech map, is similar to weaving different threads into the one cohesive fabric. The array of platforms, programming languages and frameworks form a complicated mosaic requiring a subtle approach to problem solving. What we are witnessing is artistry; the creation of an environment where

different technologies do not compete, but collaborate synergistically.

Adopting standardized communication protocols is central to this effort. This helps establish a standard language that facilitates smooth communication between various parts of the tech ecosystem. Middleware solutions play an essential role as a mediator between incompatible technologies, ensuring that they operate harmoniously. Furthermore, proper integration of APIs facilitates seamless communication between different systems as it allows them to pass data and functionality efficiently.

3. **Safeguarding the Digital Fortress**: Threat of data security becomes one critical act to fortify against. Sensitive information is stored in the digital fortress, making it an attractive target for a variety of cyber threats. Managing to cope with challenges in data security needs coordination of several lines on defense.

   Encryption protocols are the fortresses of digital protection. Implementing strong encryption ensures that sensitive data is protected from unwarranted access, making it an encrypted cipher that cannot be read by any potential hackers. Practice, regular security audits become the watchtowers providing wide view of vulnerability and potential breaches. Cybersecurity threats are constantly evolving system; hence, constant vigilance and adaptation to the dynamics of these things is called for. Continuous monitoring and optimization stands as a cornerstone pillar in any digital defense strategy because it ensures that proper steps have been taken when handling cyber security.

   The collaboration between tech and security teams becomes a vital synergy in strengthening the digital fortress. Building a common awareness of potential threats and vulnerabilities, these teams can jointly develop preventive actions to protect valuable information. The digital fortress can be so resilient not because of the technological shield but rather by people involved in its protection activities.

4. **Balancing Growth and Performance**: Scalability challenge beckons in the fast-paced tech industry where organizations fiercely pursue growth ambitions amidst unwavering performance. Effective ability to scale ensures that tech solutions will not suffer any loss in performance as the loads increase and user base change.

Often, when dealing with the scalability puzzle, architects are required to develop agile and adaptable solutions. Investing in scalable architectures especially cloud-based solutions becomes a strategic action. Cloud computing enables the scalability of resources to rise and fall dynamically based on varying workloads.

Continuous performance monitoring and optimization of such metrics become the navigation compass, helping tech teams detect bottlenecks in their processes, identify them and suppress. The model's scalability makes the mantra a pre-emptive rather than an adaptive one. Tech teams should not only react to the current preferences of customers but predict future growth curves. By considering scalability as an essential feature of the tech environment, organizations can overcome all difficulties confidently and assure that their solutions are not only able to grow but also develop in tandem with a multifaceted industry landscape.

The way to overcome the challenges of interoperability is through a never-ending creative process. Just as a master weaver creates each stitch with utmost care, tech teams need to be constantly refining and adapting. With a mindset that sees the variety of technologies not as an obstacle but as possibility for innovation they can create all threads in this tapestry which will have every thread contributing to overall richness and functionality within the tech ecosystem.

Chapter 8. Interactive Problem-Solving Exercises

Interactive problem-solving exercises have become a primary pillar for both educational projects and professional growth. These practice exercises, which are meant to immerse the participants into practical situations come with a host of benefits.

One of the major advantages concerns practical use of theoretical knowledge. Interactive activities give participants a concrete platform to put problem-solving principles into practice. This is a practical approach that not only improves their comprehension but also gives them the tools to manage complicated obstacles in professional life.

Another persuasive feature is collaborative learning. Tech projects frequently need teamwork, and interactive exercises provide students with an environment for collaboration, insight sharing, leveraging different perspectives. The collaborative environment mimics the realities of technical projects, fostering effective team communication.

Besides technical skills, these drills develop a comprehensive skill set. Participants not only improve their technical problem-solving skills but also develop interpersonal competencies including communication, empathy and active listening. As these skills are integral to the tech industry, interactive exercises cater for a full learning experience.

These exercises are further improved by including realistic simulations. By placing participants in scenarios similar to those they may face within professional spheres, such exercises allow individuals to bridge the divide between theory and practice. This practical approach ensures that participants are well-prepared for the complexity of the dynamic tech landscape.

Interactive exercises that promote a dynamic learning experience are noteworthy. Participants interact with the material in an active way, leading to a deeper comprehension of problem-solving concepts as they are applied through direct practical use. This dynamic approach not only improves immediate understanding but also helps to remember knowledge in the future.

Another advantage includes immediate feedback loops. Participants can evaluate their problem-solving strategies on the go, allowing them to improve constantly. This repetitive feedback procedure supports continuous learning and ensures that respondents can refine their strategies whenever new insights become readily available.

The strength of these exercises is that they are adaptable. Customizing the content to address specific learning goals or problems faced by participants ensures relevance and relatability in terms of addressing those individuals' unique needs. This adaptability makes it more personalized and effective, as a learning experience.

Interaction produces motivation and engagement automatically. These activities are dynamic and participatory, making the learning process a more enjoyable and effective one. Participants are not merely passive subjects but active agents of their own learning path, creating an attitude of possession and interest

Exercise 1: The Tech Scenario Workshop

At the immersive Tech Scenario Workshop, participants embark on an adventure of problem-solving by diving deep into a tech scenario or case study. These scenarios are designed carefully to show a range of difficulties and complications that one can find in the constantly changing tech sector. Participants, working either individually or through the use of groups will need to analyses each scenario in-depth.

The first goal is to utilize a systematic and strategic way of solving problems. By utilizing this multi-faceted analysis, participants develop a more comprehensive view of problem solving because they can seek solutions that do not just address the immediate issue at hand but also contribute to broader organizational objectives.

After the analysis phase, participants present structured solutions. This segment serves as not only space for sharing ideas but also forum that allows collective learning through group discussions. These discussions are enriched with the differing diverse perspectives that amplify the power of collaborative problem solving, contributing to overall learning.

The Tech Scenario Workshop does not only focus on the problem-solving skills but also facilitates thinking critically and decision making collectively. By walking through life-like situations, participants not only learn more about how to approach and solve tech problems but also become ready for the complexities of their professional lives.

Exercise 2: The Tech Hackathon

Tech Hackathon is just like a hackathon that involves high energy level bringing innovation and urgency into the room. The participants are formed into groups and each group is provided with a given problem statement that has strong pertinence to their area of specializations. The challenge is clear: Develop, implement a prototype and display an actionable solution in limited period.

Apart from testing the problem-solving capabilities of participants, this exercise also highlights important skills like time management, teamwork and innovative thinking. The hackathon being a collaborative event encourages an atmosphere in which various skill set and viewpoints can converge towards the accomplishment of common objectives. The competitive element brings an additional dimension of excitement as it replicates the real-world scenario where deadlines and innovation are synonyms.

The Tech Hackathon provides opportunities to sharpen adaptive problem solving under pressure, as teams work against the clock. Participants do not only struggle with the technical aspects of their chosen problem but also learn how to deal effectively within a restricted time-bound and dynamic setting.

Exercise 3: The Tech Innovation Symposium

Start your journey to creativity and innovation with the dynamic interactive experience of Tech Innovation Symposium – an event designed at engaging participants in the world where problems are solved by using technological innovations. This symposium emulates the pattern of a technology conference in which participants are not only problem solvers but visionary innovators.

A futuristic tech landscape characterized by emerging trends, potential disruptions and uncharted territories is presented to the participants. Their task is to identify and address the most urgent problems and opportunities in this changing environment. The symposium motivates the participants to imagine solutions that not only overcome present issues but also plan for future requirements.

The exercise takes a multifaceted approach, that is combining ideation with prototyping and strategic planning. Participants are encouraged to cooperate, utilizing the rich experience aimed at constructing new solutions. The symposium is not merely a solution to the problems at hand but makes participants more proactive people – ready for changes in tech world with an aim of being innovative and flexible.

Those activities are carefully developed to engage the participants in interactive problem-solving exercises, whereby they could practice and sharpen their abilities as if faced with similar situations during their career paths. The Tech Scenario Workshop and Tech Hackathon are dynamic tools that prepare the participants with a mindset and skills required to adapt. The Tech Innovation Symposium is not only a simulation but an encompassing event that makes people think out of the box. Participants learn how technology and innovation intersect as they become not only problem solvers but individuals who can envision what the future of technologies could be. This exercise is like a guiding star in bringing about the culture of consistent innovation within this industry.

Principle 6. Synergize Agile Soft Skills

Chapter 1. Synergizing Soft Skills in Agile Environments

Agile soft skills represent a variety of ways in which to navigate the complex morass that is agile methodology. Unlike their technical fellows, these skills go deeper into the human interfaces that inform effective collaboration, communication and problem-solving in agile environments. With the commencement of an investigation into agile soft skills, it becomes evident that their importance significantly transcends the limits stipulated by ordinary technical knowledge and is vital in determining whether agility practices succeed or fail.

The communication is the art of agility soft skills – the core element that goes beyond simple information transfer. Agile methodologies flourish in an environment where ideas, feedback and insights smoothly flow from one team member to another. In essence, effective communication in this regard means listening actively, speaking clearly and emphasizing on the ability to engage one positively.

Nowadays collaboration is a priority where communication becomes more than just an instrument; it's essence that maintains team behaviors. So, the soft skills associated with communication are not limited to transmitting ideas – they also involve subtle aspects like taking into account various perspectives, processing non-verbal signs and making sure that every member of a team's voice is heard in addition to being valued.

Essentially, agile methodologies are a symphony of collective efforts and team work comes across as the main cornerstone in this coordinated harmony. soft skills connected to teamwork go beyond the simple division of tasks; they encompass appropriate group collaboration, recognition of different expertise levels and joint dedication to common objectives. In the agile environment, good teamwork is not merely an outcome of technical competence; it arises from soft skills that can create compassion and mutual respect along with a shared mission to achieve the overall objectives of our team. Agile soft skills understand that the power of a team resides not only in its technical capabilities but even more so, where it can bring together multiple talents and perspectives effectively.

Agile methodologies are interchangeable with flexibility – the capability to work through uncertainties, thrive during change and adapt when required. In this rapidly changing terrain, where requirements are fickle and priorities may change, soft skills associated with adaptability become incredibly valuable. Individuals who have a good capacity in adaptability are better prepared to navigate through the choppy waters of agile projects.

Adaptability in the agile sense is far more than just reacting to change; it's about seeing changes as an integral part of path. Agile soft skills that develop adaptability help build a resilient team capable of facing unpredictable challenges and delivering value even in uncertain situations.

One of agile soft skills emerges emotional intelligence as the guiding force within, ensuring that human element was not forgotten among technical intricacies. Soft skills associated with emotional intelligence include self-awareness, empathy and the ability to understand other people's emotions. All these qualities help in establishing a collaborative culture where people feel noticed, recognized and empowered.

Understanding and using emotional intelligence inside agile practices is similar to opening the empathetic possibility endorsing good collaboration. But it transcends technical competence, recognizing that successful agile initiatives arise from the capacity to navigate through this subtle landscape of interpersonal relationships.

The term "synergize" in agile soft skills highlights the smooth merging of these kinds of human qualities with such principles. While methodologies offer directions and broad guidelines, it is the people along with their soft skills that bring life to these structures. When agile principles are synergized with soft skills it means that the success in practicing agile is not a matter of stiff obedience to rules, but an attitude embracing technical mindness together with human touch on collaboration.

Thus, agile soft skills are the hidden strings that run through any fabric of methods for doing Agile. They link people, facilitate collaboration and support the adaptive resilient nature of agile practices. In other words, these skills recognize that the triumph in agile passion and journey is not only by having good rules to follow but also on embracing mindset where technical knowledge goes hand-in-hand with human qualities people bring into a collaborative table.

Since organizations are constantly moving through a perpetually changing field of technology and project management, so the essential place that agile soft skills play puts in sharp focus. This is beyond project delivery; it's about building a dynamic culture where people flourish, work together seamlessly and collectively ensure the success of an entire team. Since agile methodologies offer technical orchestrations of dancing aspirants, soft skills are the beautiful dance that enhance whatever performance from mediocrity to brilliant collaborative brilliance.

At the core, synergy represents a harmonious blend of different units that working collectively have an impact equivalent to more than their individual contributions. In the world of agile methodologies which life on adaptability, collaboration and iterative progress integration of soft skills become a catalyst for this synergistic fusion. Soft skills such as Communication, Teamwork, Adaptability and Emotional Intelligence acts like glue that holds together the various talents on an agile team.

Agile practices for their iterative and collaborative nature, need a degree of collaboration that means more than simply carrying out the task. Synergy then serves as the guiding principle that helps teams go through the complexity of agile development by effortlessly combining together their various strengths. Soft skills play the role of this synergy conduit, facilitating communication routes and encouraging an environment where people understand each other well to adjust easily with such changing dynamics within a project.

Human being is often the unsung hero in relentless pursuit for agile excellence. By synergizing soft skills, it recognizes and enhances this human component as a team is more than just the whole of its technical proficiencies. It is life, an entity living on the energy of collaboration, empathy and common purpose. This recognition drives agile teams beyond basic efficiency, into a realm of creativity, resilience to overcome challenges and shared innovation.

As we seek to understand the constructive collaboration through soft skills in agile environments, leadership becomes a critical factor. Chief agile leaders move beyond the label of technical experts; they become conductors who help define an environment where soft skills are not only important but embraced. This role goes beyond the steering of a ship; it involves fostering an environment where all team member's individual soft skills harmonize to form a musical success.

In the fast-changing environment of agile practices, soft skills are considered to be one of its foundations that work towards creating a truly collaborative and adaptive atmosphere. Soft skills – the intangible threads that weave through this fabric of agile methodologies include communication, teamwork, adaptability and emotional intelligence. In order to tap into the full potential of teams and successfully navigate through the complexities of modern work methodologies, it's crucial for these soft skills to be seamlessly integrated with agile practices.

Chapter 2. Integration of Soft Skills and Agile Methodologies

Agile methodologies and soft skills, at least on the surface level appeared to be two very different terms now come together in a harmonious marriage that characterizes what it means to collaborate or manage projects effectively. In the complex terrain of agile methodologies in which adaptability, cooperation and continuity improvement prevail as kings; the amalgamation of soft skills not only facilitate achieving success but become necessary. Looking deeper into how agile methodologies and soft skills intersect, it seems that their fusion is not just a simple overlay but the harmonious merger of two entities whose combined influence accentuates each other's efficacy.

Before talking about the incorporation of soft skills, it is necessary to understand agile methodologies and their basic principles. Agile is a set of principles and values that stresses on individuals and interactions, working solutions rather than predefined process or systems. It's focused on evolving to change, gradual development and delivery of the incremental value for end–users. Agile methodologies, such as Scrum, Kanban and Extreme Programming offer frameworks or models to manage planning and development of projects consistent with these principles.

While agile methodologies offer strong frameworks for project management tools, they implicitly understand the value of human element in a collaborative process. Successful projects are never solely a matter of technical skills or adherence to process, more importantly they depend on the interactions, communication and collaboration by people involved in it.

This gives way to the incorporation of soft skills, which can be described as those interpersonal and intrapersonal qualities that are more than just technical capabilities. Soft skills include communication, collaboration, adaptability, emotional intelligence interpretation of human relationships at a wholesome level. In the world of agile methodologies soft skills help fostering a collaborative culture where effective teamwork, adaptive problem-solving and continuous improvement thrives.

Agile methodologies and soft skills play the game where each step is very complementary to another. Agile built-in priorities – individuals and interactions over processes and tools, working solutions over comprehensive documentation, customer collaboration instead of contract negotiation, respond fast change not slow adherence to plan align perfectly fine principles found in different soft skills.

Individuals and interactions hold due to the fact that effective communication among members of a particular team is highly emphasized. Communication soft skills like knowing how to listen actively and articulate your thoughts clearly conform with agile values because they enable the smooth flow of information within a team.

Strong communication is highly beneficial as Agile methodologies promote collaboration and transparency, along with the ability to adapt quickly to changing requirements. Soft skills in communication help team members to share ideas and feedback, align their efforts toward common objectives.

Agile principles emphasize close teamwork, as seen with the focus on delivering working solutions and collaboration customer. The soft interpersonal skills associated with teamwork go beyond task division to include meaningful collaboration, respect for differences of viewpoints, and joint dedication towards common goals. Combining soft skills in teamwork improves agility of methodologies by maintaining a synergistic dynamic among all members. This ability to collaborate synergistically, fully understanding each other's strengths and collectively making a commitment in the pursuit of value is such that creation aligns with the agile principles right where working solutions done as articulated prioritizing within customer collaboration.

Agile methodologies are naturally flexible, focused on the ability to respond and adapt rapidly while delivering small incremental value. As agile projects abound with uncertainties, the soft skills linked to adaptability become very important in steering through these circumstances. The combination of soft skills such as adaptability ensures that teams can adjust themselves according to changing requirements, evolving priorities and emerging issues. Strong adaptability skills of individuals promote the iterative and incremental manner of agile methodologies.

An agile principle of "customer collaboration over contract negotiation and responding to change" takes the human nature in project developments into consideration. As a vital soft skill, emotional intelligence becomes useful in analyzing and walking through the emotions of team members as well as stakeholders or end-users. There is a collaborative and supportive team culture when emotional intelligence in agile methodologies. It aids in empathy and enhances positive interactions ensuring the human element is not ignored when addressing technical complexities.

This is not just a theoretical concept, but rather something that teams and projects using successful agile methodologies experience "hands-on". In practical situations, teams who give priority to the development and nurturing of soft skills always top those that only pay attention to technical competencies. Here are some examples illustrating the concrete benefits of integrating agile methodologies with soft skills.

Agile approaches frequently use that of a Scrum Master or agile leader, who leads the team through their project lifecycle. An effective agile leader who possesses high emotional intelligence and empathy ensures that the team works cohesively. An understanding of the strengths and weaknesses of each team member, including them in appreciating their contribution to the work considered a plus for nurturing a good team atmosphere.

Agile projects are inherently flexible and can accommodate changing requirements. Teams that consider adaptability as a soft skill have no problems coping with changing priorities and an evolving project scope. People with proactive thinking, learning ability and adaptability to changing elements define the cyclically progressive nature of agile methods.

The Agile principles promote frequent collaboration with stakeholders so as to make certain that the delivered solutions agree with their requirements. The teamwork skills relevant to a collaboration with stakeholders, such as functioning well together in achieving the goals of diverse perspectives and good interpersonal relationships also increase involvement. The establishment of a unified and interactive team that works efficiently will integrate stakeholder comments without problem, resulting in more effective project outcomes.

In spite of the powerful combination that agile methodologies and soft skills offer, it also has its challenges as well considerations. Emphasis must be placed on recognizing and addressing these aspects for organizations targeting the full potential of this synergy.

Combining agile methodologies and soft skills usually involves a change of culture within organizations. This transition includes a move from being strictly process-minded to one that appreciates collaboration, adaptability, and ongoing enhancement. Ensuring a culture that supports the creation of soft skills and overcoming resistance to change can be quite difficult.

The inclusion of soft skills in agile practices require specific skill development as well training initiatives. Organizations may also need to spend funds on initiatives that promote communication, cooperation, adaptability and emotional intelligence of team members. Providing ongoing training opportunities ensures that individuals can constantly hone these skills and apply to them in the perspective of agile methodologies.

Unlike technical competencies, soft skills are difficult to measure in qualitative terms. Evaluating the effectiveness of integrating soft skills in agile practices may be difficult for organizations. It is imperative to come up with qualitative metrics and feedback systems, which measure the effects of soft skills on team collaboration successes as well as project outcomes plus stakeholder satisfaction.

It remains a constant challenge to strike the right balance between technical expertise and soft skills. Although the soft skills are vital for fruitful cooperation, a high degree of technical expertise is still essential to ensure successful project completion. Organizations must ensure that neither aspect is neglected because they are equally important for the overall success of agile efforts.

Chapter 3. Collaboration in Agile Teams

At this point, the focus is on collaboration – one of the keystones that turns agile teams into a harmonious symphony of innovation and productivity. Agile collaboration within teams is not just an act of cooperation; it's a partnership in success. This is known as the heartbeat of collaboration, and it can be seen in every stand-up session, retrospective analysis, sprint that finally creates a rhythm to move teams towards their goals. It goes beyond basic understanding. It goes beyond the provision of silos and creates a cross-functional partnership where developers, testers, designers as well as stakeholders come together.

Each member brings something different to the melody of advancement and communication becomes a concert of thought, reviews as well as inspiration.

Nonetheless, every symphony is bound to face difficulties – discordant notes that jeopardize the harmony. In terms of agile collaboration, these challenges translate to communication misunderstandings and conflicting priorities as well. Balancing between the individual autonomy and team cohesion isn't easy either.

Different tasks prioritization leads to conflicting objectives among team members. To tackle this issue, agile collaboration creates a set of distinct priorities that guarantee the uninterrupted rhythm of progress.

Individual autonomy, a principle an agile strives for, demands its synchronization with the collective story. The agile principles uphold individual freedom but the issue is to ensure this autonomy aligns with the collective story. The collaborative symphony while every musician plays their individual part must also be attuned to the overall composition.

This orchestration sees leaders and team members using tactics to ensure that collaboration remains the dominant theme. Important is the fostering of a collaborative culture; leaders create an environment in which collaboration does not imply as much obligation but that it should be celebrated norm.

Agile ceremonies – stand-ups, retrospectives, sprint planning is not such a fixation but platforms for organized lives. These ceremonies promote communication, alignment and a culture of ongoing improvement.

Cross-functional collaboration ensures every member brings their expertise, creating a richer and more nuanced composition. Effective tools make agile collaboration thrive. Digital platforms, task boards and communication channels play the role of instruments which harmonize efforts of distributed teams and increase transparency.

Riveting success stories of the collaborative symphony abound, showing how agile collaboration translates into real-world results. Spotify arranges its agile squads, tribes and guilds to facilitate cooperation across various roles.

Atlassian which powers collaboration tools such as Jira and Confluence believes in its own products. The culture they operate in is very much imbided with agile values; collaboration everything beyond geographical boundaries as well departmental silos.

The global move toward remote work has changed how people collaborate. Agile teams will handle this change by using technology to facilitate proper communication and collaboration, even when the parties involved are miles apart.

Creating a culture of collaboration is not just an aspiration; it requires conscious and continuous effort. It's about nurturing a space in which collaboration is not an oddity but the norm. It is a trip that starts with leadership, seeps through team interactions and influences every facet of organizational culture.

Leadership as the pathfinder of cultural change, has a vital role in developing a collaborative mindset. It begins with a spirit of leadership that characterizes openness, transparency and inclusivity. Leaders act as the builders of a collaborative atmosphere by demonstrating values they want their followers to adopt.

In the world of agile leadership, the path is a two-way street. Leaders establish the tone, but they also enable team members to contribute as active players in collaborative storytelling. It is a fine balancing act where leaders direct without intruding, creating an atmosphere in which every voice carries equal weight and worth. Shared responsibility is one of the main pillars that support collaborative culture, to empower teams. Shared responsibility is not only an individual being responsible for their tasks; shared means that everyone in the team should be accountable to achieve a successful job of all members. Agile teams flourish if all team members don't only own their tasks but also share overall goals for the entire team.

Communication becomes the essence of collaborative cultures. It's not only about sharing information; it is creating a mutual understanding. Agile teams use a variety of communication paths – stand-ups, retrospectives and open forums – to ensure that information flows as fast as possible so everyone can share knowledge about the context.

In this cooperative path, the idea of shared responsibility goes beyond simple activities to include knowledge exchange and skill improvement. Agile teams evolve as learning groups, where knowledge is a shared resource and skill development becomes an endeavor of all. Cross-functional collaboration makes sure that skills do not remain in the silos of two but are rather shared resources and contribute to uplift an entire team.

There are challenges in the collaborative culture too. Human interaction dynamics, conflicting priorities and diverse personalities can bring a dissonant tone to the collaborative symphony. Agile teams overcome these hurdles through empathy and active listening.

Empathy, which is one of the key elements of collaborative cultures means to understand and feel what another person feels. It's a great tool that develops mutual respect and unites opposed viewpoints. Agile leaders, constantly managing the emotional landscape of their teams' interpersonal relationships are fostering an environment where empathy is not only encouraged but it has become part innate cultural DNA.

Active listening becomes the bridge that joins team members and brings them close to similar objectives. Listening is more than just hearing sounds; it involves comprehending the underlying messages, recognizing multiple perspectives, and incorporating varied perceptions into a unified whole. Agile teams also train strongly in active listening as a core competency where every voice has an equal opportunity to contribute towards the collective conversation.

Recognizing individual and collective achievements becomes the share that strengthens ties of collaboration. Agile teams do not only value the ultimate outcomes but also highlight and celebrate their incremental wins throughout that journey. These are not the top-down gestures of recognition, but something embedded in team ethos. Agile teams develop a horizontal culture of appreciation in which every team member is valued and seen. It concerns a culture where crediting mutual responsibility becomes everybody's concern in turn.

The collaborative collaboration is not limited to the borders of a single team. It encompasses the entire organizational ecosystem at large. Agile organizations are aware that collaboration is not an isolated practice, but a comprehensive approach crossing over department levels. Departments do not work in isolation; rather they contribute to the organization's larger goals as interconnected entities.

The idea of being blame-free culture is an important thread in the tapestry of shared responsibility. Agile teams adopt the concept that failures are not setbacks but opportunities for acquiring ideas and enhancements. The spirit of shared responsibility is fostered in an environment where team members are safe to confess mistakes, share lessons learned and work collectively at learning the path to success.

It is also important to note that the collaborative ethos forms the engine room of success in agile. Encouraging a culture of collaboration and shared responsibility takes intention, leadership, as well as the collective mindset that recognizes whole power in every note played by each individual musician in an achievement symphony. As agile teams continue to evolve, the culture of collaboration is no longer a method but an emotional state – it has become inherent in their identity as organizations and helps them strive for continuous perfection.

Chapter 4. Communication and Adaptability in Agile Environments

Effective communication, which is often considered the lifeblood of any successful effort, becomes a keystone in agile setting. It is more than just the sharing of information; it is the foundation for collaboration and shared understanding within teams or groups. Effective communication is like a compass guiding the way forward in agile environments where things happen fast and landscape changes all the time.

Effective communication in agile environments is more than just message transmission at its heart. It's about developing a common ground, a universal code that runs through the heterogeneous tapestry of team members, stakeholders and users. Agile team takes a communication approach that fosters clarity, transparency and inclusivity so everyone is not just listened to but understood.

Actively listening is a quiet juggernaut in the world of effective communication. Agile teams realize that listening is not a passive activity, but an active dialog with the thoughts, doubts and suggestions of team members and stakeholders. Active listening becomes the only bridge that joins diverse views, meshing them together into a harmonious symphony of mutual comprehension.

User story is a strong narrative tool in the tapestry of agile communication. It goes beyond the confines of a requirements document becoming an alive, breathing story that reflects from the user's point of view. User stories transform agile communication into the heart of that which makes it human-centered, thereby assuring that development is not an isolated technical affair but a responsive rhythm audible to user needs and expectations.

Adaptability, which is the agile cousin of communication appears as the driving force that carries projects through unpredictable rivers of change. Adaptability in this dynamic technology and business landscape is no longer a luxury but an art of survival. Agile environments are characterized by a mindset that adapts to change, sees it not as something disruptive but an opportunity for improvement.

The agile teams recognize that the first version of a product is not an end in itself, but only one milestone on the way to constant adjustment and perfection. The agile mindset is not bound to a strict plan, but constantly adapts according to user comments, changes in the market and new opportunities.

As a result of adaptability, the MVP notion (Minimum Viable Product) takes shape in the agile environment. It is more about bringing a quick solution that satisfies the basic requirements and can continue to be developed based on real-world responses. MVP mindset reflects agility, permitting adjustments and rotations in projects based on validated learning.

Change does not always come from outside the team; it often starts within the squad. Agile environments understand that adaptability is not simply a reaction to the outside world, but an internal attitude which encourages team members for voicing ideas, challenging whatever is assumed and being actively involved in developing its own project. The adaptability of the team becomes a motive force that develops with its project.

The idea of the retrospective a key feature in agile methodology turns into a reflective space meant for adaptability. Agile Teams meet not only to discuss what was done well and wrong but also modify their processes incrementally. Retrospective is not a post-mortem but an active session where the team collectively steers in direction for continuous improvement.

Scrum framework can be recognized as a choreographer that orchestrates their harmonious integration. It provides a structured drumbeat where communication happens naturally through ceremonies such as Sprint Review, Planning and Daily Stand-ups. Scrum's iterative cycles capture the adaptable nature of it, which permits teams to inspect and adjust at frequent intervals.

Agile environments, in their quest for efficient communication and adaptability use a variety of practices as well as tools. Kanban boards serve to visualize work, ensuring transparency and promoting dialogue about the progress of tasks. Burndown charts are progress tracking, giving team members a common visual language to adjust strategies from live data.

However, communication and adaptability have its bumps. The speed at which agile projects are conducted could sometimes result in communication gaps, misunderstandings or resistance to change. Team members used to more traditional, plan-driven approaches may resist the required adaptability. Agile environments address these issues by promoting a culture of openness, learning and constant improvement.

It is time to untie the threads of success by exploring recommendations focused on improving these skills with agile teams.

Communication

- **Clear User Story Writing Guidelines**: Agile teams communicate mostly through user stories, which include the core of functionality from a point of view an end-user. It is very important to provide clear guidelines for the writing of user stories. Focus on simplicity, clarity and user orientation. Make user stories that are only technical in nature but tell a story that captivates the end-user is an art.
- **Regular Team Check-Ins**: Communication is based on the connection, and regular check-ins of a team create unity. Daily stand-ups are a quick pulse check but weekly or bi-weekly meetings provide an environment for detailed talks. These meetings should not simply be a reporting process; they should give team members enough room to air out concerns or share

insights so that the entire group works toward finding solutions. In these moments of mutual communication, the dynamics between a team get stronger.

Adaptability

- **Retrospectives for Continuous Adaptation**: Make retrospectives the foundation of the team's adaptability strategy. Open discussions about processes, tools and team dynamics should be encouraged. Therefore, this reflective practice ensures the team is not only adjusting to change but looking for ways by which they can refine and optimize their approach.
- **Iterative User Stories**: Adaptability starts with the user story. Build it to a habit of revising user stories based on the feedback from users. Agile is based on the idea of delivering value to end-users and this implies a feedback loop. By accommodating adaptability in its user story process, the team welcomes change as an avenue for continuous development. This makes each iteration one step further towards an optimized solution.
- **Digital Kanban Boards for Visual Adaptation**: Likewise, visualization is a strong asset for adaptability. The team is able to visualize the work and adjust in real-time using digital Kanban boards or task tracking tools. These tools offer a transparent vision of how the project is advancing, helping team members identify choke points and rearrange tasks or strategies quickly. At the same time, this adaptability is not merely in responding to change but anticipating it through visual signs.

Unifying Forces

- **Cross-Functional Collaboration Workshops**: The core of agile success is collaboration between technical and non-technical team members. Promote scenarios of cross-functional collaboration by hosting workshops that stimulate discussions on effective communication between different domains. These sessions should not be theoretical; rather, they must turn to practical situations that encourage a collaborative vernacular and understanding between team members who bring diverse skills.
- **Dedicated Training on Agile Principles**: True collaboration fits the core values of agile. Organize trainings on agile principles and how they influence good communication. Make sure that

team members know the importance of such principles as face-to-face communication, regular updates and a willingness to get valuable results. Such collaborative spirit prevails when everyone is attuned to these underlying and fundamental principles.

- **Leadership Role Modeling**: Leadership always plays a vital role in developing the collaborative culture of any team. Those who are leaders should demonstrate effective and transparent communication, establishing a standard that the whole team could emulate. By actively advocating for flexibility, leaders demonstrate the need to shift strategies in response to feedback and evolving circumstances.

By actively advocating for flexibility, leaders demonstrate the need to shift strategies in response to feedback and evolving circumstances. Promoting actively, adaptability leaders demonstrate the readiness to really change strategies depending on feedback and changes in circumstances.

Chapter 5. Agile Projects Innovation and Problem-Solving

Problem solving and innovation are the two engines driving agile project teams towards success. Creative problem solving and Innovation are firmly rooted in agile soft skills, which include collaboration, adaptability enhanced communication. Let's discover how these skills work together in the agile context, where challenges bloom into opportunities and innovation becomes a way of living.

Agile soft skills are catalysts for creative problem-solving. Ideation workshops highlight the power of collaboration. Agile teams flourish on diversity of thought and perspective. Conducting collaborative ideation sessions with team members from different fields offer good ground for innovative problem solving. Agile soft skill of collaboration ensures that none remains but the team's collective intelligence sets to ignite ideas.

Many agile projects require a cross-functional solution to the problems. Agile softs like collaboration and effective communication flourish by assembling teams that bring different skills sets and viewpoints to the table. As a result, these teams become microcosms of innovation and each member contributes one piece to the jigsaw puzzle of problem-solving. The agile mindset promotes ongoing feedback and improvement as the team adjusts their approach while moving closer to a solution.

The nature of agile projects is iterative, and creative problem-solving works just fine with it. Agile teams embrace the concept of fail fast, learn faster instead of waiting for a perfect solution through rapid prototyping and user testing they identify possible problems early on so that adjustments and improvements can be made quickly. An agile creative problem-solving process is essentially a constant feedback loop.

Agile soft skills are also catalysts for innovation. Innovation is not something that happens one time, but it's a continuous process. Agile soft skills help in developing a culture that is focused on continuous improvement and appreciates it. Practices such as retrospectives where teams review what was done well and things that can be improved, the agile mindset turns into an innovation driver. Each sprint presents an opportunity to fine-tune processes, experiment with different approaches and increment innovation.

A key agile soft skill is effective communication, which plays an essential role in promoting innovation. Inclusive communication gives voice to each and every team member ensuring that they feel empowered enough so as to contribute their innovative ideas. Agile projects frequently rely on teams with dissimilar skills. Open dialogue and active listening are promoted by the agile soft skills that make the environment for finding innovative solutions based on collective intelligence of members of a team.

The agile mindset, which is about being adaptable and ready for change sets the stage of innovation. In a terrain where technology and market dynamics change overnight, one's ability to adapt can be its competitive advantage. This adaptability is driven by the Agile soft skills that make teams willing to adjust strategies, entertain new technologies and see change as an opportunity for innovation rather than a challenge when it occurs.

Design thinking with an emphasis on the user reflects soft agile skills across innovation. Agile teams endeavor to make sure that their innovations match real- world needs by empathizing with end-users and including them in the design process. This approach not only improves the quality of solutions but also reduces the risk in developing products or features that might be rejected by users.

Agile projects live in the windy world of technology evolution and user expectations, therefore mastering agile soft skills is critical. These are not just means to end; they have a soul in the agile projects - they breathe life into problem-solving and ignite fires of innovation. Using the frame of agile soft skills, each problem turns into an opportunity; every sprint is trying to be as innovative canvas; and everyone project seems like a journey towards limitless opportunities provided by innovation.

Now, let's take a look at the moving stories of two real-world projects in which innovative solutions emerged as a result of agile collaboration. These narratives not only highlight the potential of agile soft skills but also reveal how an integrated, cyclical method can result in groundbreaking results.

Spotify – Changing the Way We Listen to Music

2005, the music industry faced one of its biggest problems to date rampant piracy and decline in traditional album sales. 2006, Spotify was founded to change the music streaming scene. The project targeted to develop a platform which not only facilitated users with the simplest way of accessing an enormous music library, but also helped addressing some challenges that faced the industry by presenting them on alternatives legal, easy and efficient means for everything personalized.

Spotify started with an agile approach right from the beginning. Such cross-functional teams were assembled, including software developers, designers, data analysts and music industry experts. The agile soft skills of effective communication and collaboration were essential in ensuring that each team member understood his or her role and participated towards the success of the project.

Spotify's agile journey was carried out by continuous iterations and improvements. The team was able to develop Minimum Viable Products (MVPs), which enabled users to provide early feedback, promoted a culture of adaptability. With the agile mindset, Spotify adapted when it needed to and tweaked features accordingly according to user feedback.

The outcome was an online music streaming service that surpassed user expectations, as well. Personalized playlists, collaborative playing and smart user interfaces became industry standards. With the synergy of agile soft skills, Spotify did not only resolve the problems with music industry but also opened a new chapter in how people listen to music all over the world.

Airbnb - Transforming the Hospitality Industry

Airbnb is hugely successful not only because of its business model but also it was agile. The company embraced cross-functional collaboration by getting engineers, designers and business strategists together. These diverse team members worked together, using each other's skills and perspectives.

Effective communication and empathy are some of the agile soft skills that played a crucial role. Airbnb adopted user-centered design thinking strategy by being actively involved users in the developmental process. As hosts and guests' needs and expectations continued to change, the team perfected the platform through continuous communication feedback all along.

Airbnb redefined travel and experiencing new places. These innovative features, such as user reviews, safe payment systems and a full search and booking procedure solidified the platform's success across the globe. Airbnb managed to disrupt the travel and hospitality landscape by blending agile soft skills with a community-driven ecosystem that continues to evolve on itself.

Such case studies shed light on the potential effects of agile collaboration and soft skills. Spotify and Airbnb show how a fluid, evolving, and collaborative way of thinking informed by agile values can result in revolutionary inventions that transform whole sectors.

Chapter 6. Continuous Improvement in Agile Soft Skills

The agile methodologies and the soft skills necessary for success in dynamic workplaces can be based on principles of continuous improvement. In the realm of agile methodologies, continuous improvement is not just a procedure but an attitude that influences how teams conduct their operations. In the field of soft skills, as well, continuous improvement is an endless journey in terms of personal and professional development.

The concept of continuous improvement can be linked to agile methodologies that are cyclical and iterative in nature. Agile practitioners follow principles that emphasize agility, teamwork, and flexibility to change. The Agile Manifesto is a manifest guiding the development of agility – it emphasizes people and interactions, working solutions over processes and tools. This culture of flexibility paves the way for a philosophy of continuous improvement.

The soft skills, which is also called the interpersonal or people's skill set that is tied up with technical expertise in agile teams. These skills include communication, teamwork, flexibility and problem-solving ability. Acknowledging their key function, technology industry professionals realize that soft skills mastery is not a static success – it takes constant aware and active work.

The need to continually improve is emphasized by the recurrent retrospectives that are conducted in each iteration or sprint ending. These retrospectives provide a separate time for teams to assess their performance and determine areas of improvement while making changes in the following cycles. An iterative approach means that the team is always learning, adjusting and growing.

Even when it comes to the realm of soft skills, there is a need for constant development. Essential soft skills such as effective communication demand continuous improvement. The communication modes changes with the advancement in technology. Competency is based on the level of adaptation that professionals apply to new tools, platforms, and methods in communication. Ongoing development of communication skills requires one to keep abreast with industry trends, solicit feedbacks from the surroundings and make adjustments in order to improvise.

The other important soft skill that is closely related to continuous improvement is adaptability. Within the current fast-moving technology environment, individuals are required to be flexible in their mentalities and modes of operations. It then becomes a habit of embracing change, with the commitment to continuous improvement ensuring that people remain flexible to new challenges.

Continuous improvement aids problem-solving, which is at the heart of agile methodologies and soft skills. Each problem solved within a technical project or even in an environment where one is working with others becomes a source of knowledge. Regarding problem-solving strategies, searching for alternative solutions and ensuring that successes as well as failures show improvement rendering an appropriately skilled individual or team.

A soft skill that often gets underestimated in the culture of agile is leadership which endures on a commitment to continuous improvement. Effectiveness for agile leaders is not a talent that they are born with but something that undergoes constant improvement through experience, feedback and orientation to lifelong learning. It mimics the conduct of continuous improvement, with their staff engaging in a similar mindset.

In agile methodologies and soft skills, continuous improvement is a cyclic process. It is characterized by self-awareness, feedback mechanisms and a growth mindset. The path to continuous growth involves refining coding practices, increasing cooperation in cross-functional teams or changing styles of leadership for agile practitioners and people who promote soft skills too.

Indeed, the issue of continuous improvement cannot be overestimated in agile methodologies and soft skills. It is a unifying force between the technical and interpersonal features of tech. Through shaping the culture of sustainable development, professionals guarantee their longevity and relevancy amidst constant changes. Continuous improvement is not a strategy; it's way of being within the agile and soft skills world that drives individuals and teams to sustainable success.

With professionals facing the challenges of developments in agile methodologies and soft skills, they require resilient tools and frameworks for continuous development. These tools are guiding lighthouses which help the individuals and teams to pursue more refinement and perfection.

An example of a continuous improvement tool for agile methods is the Lean methodology, especially Kanban. From the manufacturing field, Kanban has found its way for application in software development and project management. Indeed, it can help visualize the process of work as it flows through a system and enable teams to locate blockages while improving efficiency by streamlining workflows. The Kanban board can be a visual example of tasks that become the presentation of workload in progress. With Kanban adoption, teams are capable of making constant process improvements that respond to changes quickly and improve collaboration.

Ongoing development tools can also be used by agile frameworks such as Scrum. Sprint Retrospectives are a fundamental feature of the Scrum methodology that enables teams to evaluate their work. In facilitated sessions, team members can reflect on what went right and wrong in the light of improving their work jointly. This iterative feedback loop ensures that the team is constantly improving its practices, responding to emerging threats and creating a continuous improvement culture.

As concerns with regard to soft skills particularly communication and working together, one potent framework used is the NVC model of Nonviolent Communication. Need-based communication method, NVC was designed by Marshall Rosenberg. It promotes attentive listening and the use of 'I' statements to communicate feeling or thought without passing judgement. This framework encourages open and constructive communication promoting continuous enhancement in interpersonal skills.

Another effective soft skills development tool is the Growth Mindset, created by psychologist Carol Dweck. A growth mindset is characterized by viewing challenges as potential areas of development and the belief that skills can be acquired over time. This change in mindset is an effective tool for the virtue of continuous improvement, whereby people perceive difficulties as opportunities to adapt and see learning as a lifelong process.

Therefore, feedback mechanisms have a central part in the continuous improvement of both agile methodologies and soft skills. Tools for 360-degree feedback used in conjunction with performance management systems enable individuals to gather information from their peers, superiors and subordinates. Indeed, such a holistic feedback loop provides an all-inclusive perspective on one's strengths and opportunities for advancement that enable focused growth endeavors.

Coding dojos come in handy as an interactive and collaborative learning environment for developing technical skills of agile teams. A coding dojo is a practice in which team members meet to work on challenging problems and exchange ideas, as well as learn. This experiential learning not only builds necessary technical skills but also fosters a culture of ongoing improvement.

In the domain of leadership, frameworks such as Situational Leadership model help provide a way for leaders to incorporate their approach into changing based on team members' maturity and competency. This resilient leadership practice is consistent with the culture of continuous improvement where leaders are encouraged to assess, review and modify their plans in accordance with new circumstances.

Finally, development and refinement are navigable with the help of these tools and frameworks which act as compass to direct each individual or team towards perfection. These tools equip professionals with the ability to embrace change, promote a culture of teamwork and develop an attitude towards constant improvement. Through the application of these instruments into their day-to-day activities, practitioners from tech industry can overcome constant changes in this world carrying agility genuineness and perpetual growth.

Chapter 7. Interactive Agile Soft Skills Workshop

This intersection of agile methodologies and soft skills is one that many are dubbing the focal point. The synergy between these two realms is not only an abstract theory but a power that drives teams into innovation, cooperation and project completion. To supplement this constructive collaboration, interactive workshops offer readers a hands-on approach that allows them to experience firsthand how interchangeable these principles are in practical application.

Interactive Workshop 1: The Agile Soft Skills Simulation

The workshop starts with an interesting opening that introduces the participants. Teams of attendees are formed that reflect the cross-functional nature commonly present in tech application. All teams get a case study corresponding to common situations that occur within the tech field, including draconian timelines; changing priorities and communication lapses.

Participants move through iterations of simulation by going from one round to another. Scenarios undergo changes, and team have to adapt promptly. Instead, there is a focus on soft skills that are agile-based – such as effective communication, teamwork cooperation and adaptability problem solving. Facilitators introduce surprises and change, making teams rethink strategies and utilize their soft skills toolbox.

Active involvement is promoted in the simulation where team members perform different roles to learn about various aspects of agile and soft skills. For instance, one member of the team may act as a product owner while another acts as developer and yet another is scrum master. This rotation promotes an overall comprehension of the challenges that are prevalent in various positions with regards to a project.

After the round of simulations, a detailed debriefing meets. Facilitators lead participants into exploring their experience, pointing out what went right as well as where obstacles lie. This reflective process stresses the frequency of improvement and how practicing agile soft skills enables better teamwork and project results.

The workshop ends with a section on deriving main points. The identified insights are actionable by the participants enough that they can use it in their real-world projects. This could entail embracing more open lines of communication, conducting frequent retrospectives or promoting a team that takes part in problem-solving as teams. The objective is for each participant to apply learned strategies in their work environment that will improve the individual's agile soft skills.

Interactive Workshop 2: The Cross-Functional Collaboration Challenge

In this workshop, participants learn how to solve a cross-functional collaboration challenge. So, attendees are divided into mixed teams that consist of people with various skill sets – just like tech projects today.

The teams are given a complex problem or goal of the project which needs to be solved using cross-functional team contributions. Each round of the challenge reveals a new aspect of the problem. Slowly, the teams can utilize their soft skills to counter this challenge. Facilitators behave as stakeholders and introduce new demands or restrictions to mimic real-life project operation.

The workshop motivates groups to find win-win alternatives. Negotiation, compromise and the need for effective communication become integral part of the challenge. The iterative nature of the rounds follows the agile approach where there is a continuous cycle that are geared with adaptability and constant improvement.

After the challenge rounds, participants take part in a debriefing and reflection session. This is done through the facilitators who steer discussions of collaborative strategies focusing on how to understand different viewpoints and arrive at solutions that benefit everyone.

To wrap up the workshop, participants synthesize main insights from the challenge. Focus is on practical aspects of these realization in the course of their practice, providing a more integrative problem-solving. Participants also join the workshop with appreciation for teamwork and an arsenal of tactics used in agile soft skills.

Interactive Workshop 3: Proactive Communication Clinic

The topic of this workshop is proactive communication as one example among other agile soft skills. In such scenarios, immersed participants communicate openly and in timely manner. The session starts off by analyzing the importance of proactive communication in Agile settings.

Teams are presented with virtual communication barriers replicating real-life situations. These issues may be due to a distributed team, cultural differences or time zones. Proactive communication strategies such as regular stand-ups, transparent documentation and proactive issue escalation is displayed actively among the participants. The adaptability and creativity of the teams are tested with every new challenge, which is to preserve efficient channels for communication.

After the challenge, a detailed debriefing session takes place. Facilitators help participants reflect on the communication techniques used, and identify effective practices. This reflective process brings out the cyclic attributes of communication in agile environments.

The end of the workshop is marked with participants summarizing important lessons on proactive communication. The practical insights gained from the challenges are also presented, and they agree on actionable recommendations aimed at improving their proactive communication skills within agile teams. This workshop provides the tools that participants need to effectively communicate in agile settings.

Workshop 4: Innovation Sprint

This workshop immerses the group into an innovative world of problem-solving in agile structures. First, the focus is on determining how establishing a culture of innovation correlates with agile practices.

Teams go through a sequence of innovation challenges in which they must come up with innovative answers to difficult problems. The challenges are meant to surpass the given limitations in thinking so that one can combine agile methodologies with innovative problem-solving. Facilitators present limitations and disturbances in order to replicate the unstable nature of tech projects.

Teams fully accept the agile principle of change and consider difficulties as prospects for innovation. The iterative nature of agile methodologies also manifests itself in the ongoing improvement in solutions through subsequent cycles.

After the innovation challenges, there is a debriefing session. The facilitators take participants through reflecting on the creative problem-solving approaches used. The conversations focus on how promoting innovation within agile teams not only addresses current challenges, but also creates a culture of permanent change and adaptation.

At the end of this workshop, participants will identify critical things associated with promoting innovation in agile settings. In the challenges, findings from insights gained are discussed by participants and actionable strategies to introduce creativity in their everyday work. This workshop arms participants with the right attitude and tools to ingrain innovation into their agile transformation story.

These interactive workshops act as furnaces where theory and practice meet. Learners get not only to understand how agile and soft skills can be synergize but also see their transforming effects on practice. Through practice in the simulations and challenges faced, they optimize their skills to handle the dynamics of technicians. The workshops act as catalysts for organizational cultural changes, resulting in a mindset that embraces the concept of continuous improvement; collaboration and ubiquitous integration of agile methodologies with soft skills.

Continuous improvement is not just a process idea and methodology, but indeed in people's personal development. In the world of agile soft skills, continuous improvement is an ongoing personal journey requiring introspection and goal-setting. Self-reflection is a foundation of continuous improvement. It is the compass that leads people across their map of talents, helping them discover strengths, weaknesses and untapped resources. This reflective process in an agile soft skills backdrop makes people recall past conversations, analyze communication manners and styles, collaboration routines thus solving issues.

With the help of real-life situations, people can make sense of their experiences in order to identify occasions that they succeeded and those where shortcomings should be identified. This transformation not only highlights the complexity of soft skills but also fosters a better understanding as to how these characteristics impact or diminish agile methodologies.

The next phase or stage after the terrain has been surveyed through self-reflection is then plotting a strategy for improvement. Setting of goals in agile soft skills is a careful and thoughtful action. It focuses on the preparation of SMART objectives related to agile methodologies.

Goals may include improving communication effectiveness and creating a more collaborative team environment, as well refining problem-solving skills and the embracing of adaptability. The main thing is to modify such targets in accordance with one's specific situation within the agile setting. In this way, people not only establish the path to progress but also support collective improvement and flexibility of agile team.

When combined with peer cooperation, the continuous improvement trip gathers speed. Agile soft skills cannot stand alone but need the cross – connections from a team. Through peer feedback, growth is accelerated through other angles of articulation different from those that might be mentioned during individual self-reflection.

Having open and constructive conversations with peers helps people to comprehend how others perceive their soft skills within the dynamics of a team. It nurtures a culture of building on strengths and makes challenges a shared opportunity for betterment. This interdependence culture reflects agile practices such as teamwork, iterative advancement and joint responsibilities.

It should also be noted that evolutionary development is not limited to one-time, but such a principle is rooted in the very agile philosophy. It converts individual career of growth into group project, where each member plays an important role in the dynamic development for entire team.

Through creating an environment that celebrates self-awareness, intentional goal setting and teamwork learning agile members become robust in nature. The continuous improvement process is inherently iterative, and it meshes perfectly with agile methodologies to form a mutually beneficial relationship between personal growth and the triumphs of pursuing an agility agenda. This is where the individual growth meets teamwork alignment, and this agile sprit captures where teams strive for superiority in a rapidly changing world of technology.

Principle 7. Sharpen the Soft Skill Saw

Chapter 1. Overview of Continuous Soft Skill Development

The phenomenon of "sharpening the saw in terms of soft skills" proves itself an effective strategy that can be used by tech companies to further improve their activities. Soft skills, which oftentimes serves the central role in communication and collaboration as well problem-solving should repeatedly be perfected to remain up to standard. This principle involves actively improving one's soft skills, since polishing the tool increases its effectiveness.

To realize the core of sharpening a soft skill saw, one should imagine it as complex tool like a saw. This tool, if properly maintained and sharpened becomes better equipped to fight obstacles and complexities. The analogy highlights that, as a saw must be sharpened from time to time for it remain effective so soft skills should often get attention and be developed periodically. The soft skill saw has several other features that include communication, teamwork, flexibility, problem solving and leadership. All elements contribute to the tool's precision, allowing people using them not only to survive but also enjoy navigating in and around tech industry machinations.

When in a technological world where change is the only constant, there emerges an obvious need to develop soft skills constantly. With innovations in technology, multicultural teams as well as changing project requirements demand an agile and adaptive workforce. Soft skills referred to as the pillars of successful technology projects have a significant function in navigating them through these turbulent obstacles.

In this meaning, continuous development includes active learning, purpose of practice and a developing mentality. It demands constant awareness of new trends, suggestions from others and experiential knowledge. The ultimate goal is not just competence but mastery – a continuous endeavors of constantly refining and expanding one's inventory of soft skills.

The constantly changing nature of the tech industry requires a set of soft skills that can keep up with this speed. Alignment of these soft skills with the dynamic technological environment is needed for honing the saw. For example, in time new methods of communication are developing and people should learn how to use their communicative abilities effectively for virtual collaborations and distributed teams. One of the most important soft skills, adaptability plays a key role in helping people get used to new technologies and techniques. Constant integration maintains that soft skills not only keep up with technological change but also serve as drivers of effective tech implementation and innovation.

The sharpening of the soft skill saw thus goes far beyond individual efforts; it entails creating a culture of continual learning among tech teams and organizations. This cultural change requires acknowledging that soft skills are not hard-fixed attributes but fluid capabilities which flourish in cultures of discovery, cooperation and ongoing improvement. Organizations foster an atmosphere that encourages individuals to begin on learning voyages, impart experiences and mentor others. In turn, this collaborative approach facilitates the collective sharpening of a soft skill saw that improves teams' performance and promotes resilient adaptive organizational culture.

Those organizations and individuals that focus on continuous soft skill development are seen as agile tech players. The eternally-keen soft skill saw becomes a metaphor for adaptability, teamwork and the pledge to mastering technology's nuanced complexities with sharpness. As technological changes become increasingly complex, those who address sharpen their soft skill saw are in a better position to withstand the dynamics of change but also build on it.

The importance of continued progress and improvement in soft skills within the professional realm cannot be underestimated. With the dynamics of near to human-like industry transformations due to technological and workplace revolutions, soft skills become increasingly necessary. Soft skills need to be constantly improved throughout the individual career path, team development, and organizational achievements.

Nowadays, soft skills become an essential tool for success in the professional environment dominated by advanced automation where work can be performed remotely and markets are globalized. Softer skills such as interpersonal communication, collaboration among teammates and adaption to a variety of workplace cultures have now become equally important as technical expertise. Soft skills become catalysts for innovation as industries develop, resulting in the integration of new technologies that subsequently lead to organizations' development.

The modern model of the workplace requires regular learning. Soft skills revolving around emotional intelligence, adaptability and the ability to communicate with other people change on an ongoing basis to keep in line with a rapidly changing professional world. A combination of technological competence and well-developed soft skills makes people flexible workers who contribute to organizational objectives.

The importance of soft skills in promoting teamwork and realistic dynamics cannot be overstated within the work cultures involving teams commonly practiced across many industries. Sustained advancements in these disciplines improve not just the individual contributions but also teamwork performance. Collaboration is based on openness of communication, active listening and empathetic understanding - all these are soft skills. Soft skill enhancement remains integral to a positive team culture, built upon appreciation of different perspectives and constructive conflict resolution. Members of the team who have developed their soft skills are specialists in networking, interpersonal conflict resolution and building a sense of purpose. This ethic serves as an anchor to meet the project objectives and overcome challenges brought by complicated work environments.

Adaptability is a fluid trait that needs to be constantly sharpened. Those professionals who focus on continuous development in soft skills turn into flexible contributors that adapt quickly to changing trends, technological conditions, structural modifications. In a world where change is the only constant, adaptability becomes differentiating.

This importance of continuous improvement in soft skills does not stay at the level of individual contribution to achieving overall success for organizations. Organizational effectiveness is heavily dependent on leadership, which itself relies extensively upon the soft skills. The leaders who constantly develop their communication, emotional intelligence and conflict resolution abilities stimulate such environment wherein employees feel appreciated as well as driven.

The success of an organizational unit depends on the cumulative soft skills that make up its workforce. A culture of continuous improvement in these areas leads to innovation, resilience and healthy workplaces. Additionally, top managers who focus on the steady development of soft skills become role models for others what impacts not only their own behavior but also an entire culture in a company.

The spotlight on continuous soft skills development and improvement is crucial in the modern workplace environment. Soft skills bundled as such become cornerstones of success as industries develop, workplaces change and the quality of teamwork changes paradigm. People, teams and organizations acknowledging the need to consistently refine soft skills not only become change-resilient but serve as agents of positive renewal.

Chapter 2. The Changing Nature of Tech and Soft Skills

The tech sector is a bold and always changing world defined by changes, radical conceptions transformative developments. However, in this vibrant setting the interdependent character of technological excellence and soft skills has become more obvious. This essay tackles the changes in technology sector and its impact on soft competencies of experts that are required to do their job.

The rate of technological advancements in the tech sector is unprecedented. From AI to the ongoing honing of cybersecurity efforts, this sector is ever evolving. In this dynamic field, shifting from the sole emphasis on technical skill to a more balanced focus that takes into account so called soft skills has become inevitable.

The emergence of interdisciplinary collaborations and cross-functional teams in technology companies highlights the need for communication, collaboration, and adaptability. As the technologies grow more sophisticated and projects become increasingly complicated, this kind of ability to dislodge ideas as well as work with various people perfectly is a necessity for successful performance. Soft skills, commonly called the human aspect of technology drive tech projects and whether tech-based organizations would be successful or not. The distinction between technical and interpersonal dynamics has inevitably been blurred, superseded by the need for professionals who can master both fields with elegance.

In the current tech environment, the multifaceted problems that professionals tackle are not only limited to coding and algorithm design. Complex problem-solving involves both technical skills and the ability to understand user needs, foresee challenges in advance, as well as communicate solutions clearly. The emergence of user-centric design thinking has enhanced the importance of empathy and understanding users in designing effective tech solutions that truly speak to people.

On the other hand, the advent of remote work, accelerated by global events, has amplified the need for soft skills in fostering virtual collaborations. Tech teams working in distributed environments need professionals who are able to create a team spirit, communicate well, and manage cultural differences effectively; that's why such workers become precious assets.

Soft skills are no longer complementary to the technical expertise; they have already become an indispensable part of tech culture. This is because traditional hierarchies are breaking down in favor of more egalitarian and collaborative approaches where leadership no longer rests exclusively on technical aptitude, but rather effective inspiration to drive a team towards change.

Emotional intelligence is an essential competency for tech leadership. The capacity to comprehend and manage one's own and other people's emotions is a priceless skill that promotes the development of positive working conditions, conflict resolution, as well as inspiring innovation. Strong emotional intelligence among leaders enables them to guide their teams through challenges with resilience and foster a culture of cultivating perpetual improvement.

This changing landscape has ramifications in the field of tech education and professional development as well. Educational programs are redefining their curricular to accommodate a broad range of skills, acknowledging the fact that tomorrow's workforce will require both technical proficiency and soft-skills capabilities. However, professionals are beginning to understand the importance of continuous learning not only in order to keep up with new technologies but also for developing an expanded repertoire of soft skills tools.

Today the tech industry already is no longer a field that belongs solely to lonely introverts coding in solitude. The narrative now goes into tandem with collaboration, innovation and a realization that the best tech solutions are those which perfectly balance technological genius along with an insightful understanding of human requirements as well.

As the tech industry forges ahead relentlessly, soft skills will continue to be at its center of development. The successful tech professionals of this changing world will be those who can effectively communicate complex technical information in an understandable manner, collaborate across diverse groups and environments while responding to continuous changes. This is the dawn of a new age in tech, where human-centricity and technological advancement are indissolubly tied together; where soft skills not only become an asset but necessary conditions for meaningful and sustainable success.

It is no longer just a recommendation for tech specialists to remain relevant; rather, this process should be considered integral. The unwavering speed of technological evolution, as well as the volatile nature in terms of industry trends requires proactive and ongoing learning process.

Maintaining a trend in the technology world entails updating trends, innovations that are on rise and new technologies. This implies that tech professionals have to be involved in continuous research, they should attend the conferences practice webinars and inhabit into immense knowledge pools floating around. At the same time, deep familiarity with programming languages, frameworks or advanced tools and commitment to stay current is a basic prerequisite.

However, adaptability is not only about assimilating new technical skills. It entails an approach that is open to changing, looks forward adversities and prosper in volatile settings. Agility does not only concern learning the newest high-level programming language; it also relates to adapting fast and adjusting shifting project needs, industry trends as well as overall technology environment.

In the case of paradigm shifts in industry, there is a clear need for adaptation. For example, the advent of cloud computing, convergence with artificial intelligence and increasing focus on cybersecurity have changed job skills. In this respect, tech specialists that are capable of embracing such shifts place themselves not only as contributors but leaders behind the transformative initiatives within their organizations.

Continuous learning platforms, online courses and certifications are now indispensable tools for tech professionals to ensure constant upgrades of their cognitive flexibility. This has made it easier for people to learn new skills, develop those they already have and keep an eye on latest industry practices. Professionals that connect with these platforms show a willingness to invest in themselves and their careers.

Networking is also crucial for staying abreast and adjustable. Peer interactions, industry events attendance and commenting in online forums allow sharing ideas with like-minded people or discover knowledge beyond classroom fences. Networking allows a person to both gain new ideas and work with those that share similar interests during change.

The continuous change of the tech industry requires a mindset that constantly learns and adapts. This pledge is not only for the purpose of staying current in the job market but also a vital force behind innovation and success. Through embodying the culture of progress, tech professionals are turning into incredible assets for their organizations and help to improve innovation as a whole. In an industry where standing still is certainly not a viable option, this call to stay current and evolve goes beyond the realm of professional responsibility; it becomes a strategic demand for continued success and relevance.

Chapter 3. Identifying Personal Soft Skill Gaps

The process of identifying personal soft skill gaps is an important step along the way to continuous improvement and professional development. A comprehensive self-assessment helps people understand their strengths, weaknesses and improvement opportunities clearly. Here are practical steps and guidance for self-assessment.

1. **Soft Skills Self-Assessment Questionnaire.** Develop a comprehensive questionnaire dealing with the wide range of soft skills essential to career achievement. For communication, ask about verbal and written skills along with active listening abilities as well as clarity of expression. Focus on collaboration by examining teamwork, conflict resolution and compatibility across different groups. For adaptability, consider the ability of respondents to deal with change in terms of changes and ambiguities facing them as well as those unplanned challenges that often come their way. Also, discuss leadership and interpersonal skills. Administer a Likert scale or numerical rating system for each skill's self-perceived competency. It is also advisable to use open-ended questions that push for thoroughly detailed responses, which provide qualitative information on contexts where the attributes were used.

2. **Reflective Journaling with STAR Technique**. Readers keep a reflective journal based on the STAR method, an organized way of relating events. Encourage them to give a description of the Situation – Task – Action – Result for each entry, with focus on soft skills that they used when in such situations. The purpose of this exercise is to act as a type of dynamic self-reflection tool that will allow people to look at and analyses their behavioral responses in different professional environments. By using the STAR technique, participants develop a deeper understanding of their own behavior with insights into how soft skills work and where improvement may be needed.

3. **360-Degree Feedback Exercise**. The 360-degree feedback exercise involves gathering various perspectives, enabling a broader look at an individual's soft skills. Prepare a detailed template that must have questions targeted to various aspects of communication, cooperation, flexibility and leadership. Ask participants to ask for feedback from different sides such as colleagues, leaders, subordinates and even external contacts. Highlight the value of anonymity to ensure truthful and helpful criticism. This exercise not only helps people become more aware but also shows the differences between a person's self-perception and someone else vision. The collected insights can contribute as a valuable input to targeted skill development.

4. **Behavioral Interview Simulation**. Construct an interactive environment based on a behavioral interview of participants projected in realistic situations closely related to their working life. Design questionnaires in the form of specific tools based on situational prompts that require soft skills such as conflict resolution, pressure decision-making or crisis communication. Let the participants react as they would in a typical situation. After finishing the simulation, organize a debriefing session where they can reflect on their reactions and identify patterns as well as areas that need improvement. This practical exercise increases the self-awareness aspect of a soft skill with actionable outcomes offering tips for improving soft skills in real life situations.

5. **Peer Mentoring Circles**. Support peer mentoring circles where small groups of participants share their soft skills journeys. Promote the sharing of personal experiences, challenges endured and lessons learned. Through productive peer discussions, one can acquire different perspectives. Assign

soft skill themes to each session in order that exploration is undertaken with clear direction. Peer mentoring circles create a sense of community, thus encouraging participants to share strategies and offer advice on how one would go about enhancing certain soft skills.

6. **Structured Feedback Workshops**. Arrange structured feedback workshops where participants discuss reciprocity during peer-to-peer sessions. Provide instructions and templates for giving positive feedback while also pointing out shortcomings. There should be rotating participants to get exposure different views. This recursive manner enables people to get particular feedback on soft skills from various perspectives, emphasizing the consistency of patterns and areas Structured feedback workshops foster an environment of reciprocity growth and offer pragmatic tips on how to improve soft skills collectively.

These tools collectively are designed to guide readers through a systematic and knowledgeable self-evaluation process. Through the integration of quantitative metrics, qualitative narratives, and external perspectives individuals can understand their soft skills relative composition providing them with a basis for deliberate yet effective improvement activities.

Chapter 4. Creating a Personal Development Plan

The need for ongoing improvement and development has never been greater especially when it comes to soft skill acquisition in the swift field of technology. The establishment of a detailed and personalized PDP (Personal Development Plan) is the guiding principle for all professionals aiming at reinforcing their soft skills on an ongoing basis. This five-step plan takes soft skills identification a step further to present clear instructions on how goals can be set, resources utilized well and progress followed.

1. **Identification of Soft Skills by Self-Assessment**. An effective PDP must be based on a self-discovery journey. People should conduct a holistic evaluation to draw on the wisdom from personal life and work. In doing so, one can identify certain soft skills that are central to the successful pursuit of a

career. Either it is about leadership, communication skills, adaptability or emotional intelligence – the first step includes identifying strengths and weaknesses in need of improvement.

2. **Setting Clear and Measurable Goals**. Having a comprehensive definition of today's soft skills, the further step is to develop precise and quantifiable objectives. Utilizing the SMART criteria (Specific, Measurable, Achievable, Relevant and Time-based), people can convert their unclear goals into achievable ones. For example, if the objective is to improve leadership capability, a SMART goal could look like this: "Lead an interdisciplinary project team that results in 15% improved efficiency of delivery within six months."

3. **Defining Actionable Steps**. Goals, even fully articulated ones, are dreams without accompanying action plans. Transforming each goal into specific tasks creates a plan for practical development. Still using the leadership example, specific actions could include gaining insight by attending leadership workshops; seeking guidance through a mentorship program with an established leader or participating in a smaller team project. Such steps make aspirations practical and achievable.

4. **Leveraging Learning Resources**. The contemporary professional world provides a wide array of learning opportunities for cultivation in soft skills. Individuals need to create a custom collection of resources from online courses and workshops, industry-specific forums, networking events based on their objectives. There are platforms such as Coursera, LinkedIn Learning, and industry conferences that provide worthwhile information on how to sharpen some soft skills.

5. **Progress Tracking and Adaptation**. Key to the success of every PDP is a reliable progress monitoring system. It is recommended that professional areas specify what measurement, indicators and stages will be used to evaluate progress towards each goal. This may include self-reflection, getting comments from colleagues and supervisors or measurable results at work. This step necessarily incorporates periodic reviews and adaptations, which make the PDP a dynamic document that continuously responds to changing career dreams.

Strategies for Progress Tracking:

- Regular Check-Ins: Schedule timely personal reflection sessions to measure progress and change implemented strategies.
- Feedback Mechanisms: Seek peer, mentor or supervisor feedback actively in order to receive external perspective.
- Quantifiable Metrics: Define metrics that provide measurable evidence of progress.
- Adjustment Periods: Plan for periodic reviews of the PDP, accommodating changes as appropriate.
- Celebrate Milestones: Recognize and reward success, reinforcing positive conduct.

So, by undertaking these five steps professionals can create an extensive and adaptive PDP thus being a proactive approach to the fragmented landscape of soft skill development in tech. This combination of goal-setting practices, actionable steps, supporting learning assets and proper progress monitoring helps people determine their way during the ongoing change process that shapes today's work environment.

Chapter 5. Learning from Industry Trends

The tech industry is synonymous with constant transformation as breakthroughs and innovations define this professional environment. In this dynamic situation, soft skills have come out as important constituents of success. It is becoming increasingly obvious to the specialists who work inside of tech that soft skills need not only development but further perfecting so as they can support technical prowess.

The ubiquity of technology creates today's society has brought a paradigm change in terms of what skills are needed for professionals that have moved beyond traditional technical competencies. If the professional knowledge remains core, employers value soft skills for efficient teamwork allowing easy communication and adaptation. In the process of looking at today's trends in industry, several dominant themes are identified.

Soft skills within the tech industry mark a paradigm shift in traits that are desired virtues among professionals. As technical knowledge serves as a fundament, not only this approach is coming into focus in the industry where interpersonal skills are valued for facilitating collaboration and effective leadership as well at being able to adapt. With the dynamic landscape, the tech professionals are required as not only effective in coding or technical design but also possess rich soft skills that contribute to a team's success or project and help organizations thrive in an ever-changing world. Technological developments will only lead to the emergence of synergy between technical expertise and soft skills as an aspect identifying strong professionals who have a solid foundation in technology.

Soft skill development in tech professionals is critical for keeping up with industry trends and staying informed. In the rapidly changing world of technology, success rests on being quick to respond to new developments and meeting shifting needs. Soft skills are essential in the current professional landscape that has first been overlooked but is now of crucial importance.

While constant learning is essential for the tech industry, having a feel of soft-skill trends cannot be overlooked. The study of soft skills in the tech environment helps people understand what is considered and where it demands. This knowledge acts as a navigational instrument for creating individual development plans and fine-tuning the areas in accordance with industry guidelines.

A notable trend is the growing focus on emotional intelligence. With technology infiltrating human experiences, professional have to be equipped with the capacity for interaction within socially intricate environments. Emotional intelligence deals with the ability to control one's feelings and also to interpret others' emotions and manipulate their mood states. This tendency shows people's increasing awareness of the fact that technical skills are not enough for success; harmonious interaction and partnership presuppose high emotional intelligence level.

Another worthy trend is flexibility. Since the rate of technological change is getting faster, professionals have to develop a way of thinking that embraces changes. Adaptability includes being willing to change, learning rapidly and modifying with shifting circumstances. Adaptability in the context of soft skills is now associated with resilience and resourcefulness.

Moreover, the spirit of collaboration is gaining popularity. Days of techie seclusion are numbered as professionals are called on to cross boundaries among disciplines without a hitch. Collaboration is not limited to technical teams that work with colleagues from marketing, finance etc. in other departments. A nurtured collaborative mindset includes effective communication, active-listening skills and an openness to accept the views of others.

Knowing these trends gives the professionals working in tech a guide for their continuous improvement. With awareness of the changing needs in an industry, employees can consciously put their efforts into obtaining soft skills that differentiate them from others. Not just in terms of staying current, but leading the way toward mastering those very disciplines that will establish a trend for future tech professionals.

Finally, the tech industry's always-evolving nature requires active soft skill training. Therefore, keeping abreast of developments in the industry is not simply a passive observation – it is an active tactic to navigate one's career. Embracing the current trends in EQ, adaptability and collaborative powers helps tech professionals be ahead of their development journey; staying agile flexible to take advantage or workaround different situation.

Chapter 6. Professional Development Resources

A path of ongoing development to focus on soft skills requires the availability of important resources that can support and enrich learning. This list serves as a guide to resources that are recommended for further professional development, ranging from books and courses. The rich variety of these resources means that learners with different learning preferences, whether online or offline, will have ways available for fulfilling their needs.

Books:
1. **"Emotional Intelligence" by Daniel Goleman:** This classic work explores the concept of emotional intelligence and its significance in personal and professional success. Goleman's insights provide a foundational understanding of the importance of emotions in the workplace.

2. **"Atomic Habits" by James Clear:** Soft skill development often involves cultivating positive habits. Clear's book delves into the science of habit formation, offering practical strategies for building and sustaining habits that contribute to personal and professional growth.
3. **"Crucial Conversations: Tools for Talking When Stakes Are High" by Kerry Patterson, Joseph Grenny, Ron McMillan, and Al Switzler:** Effective communication is a cornerstone of soft skills. This book equips readers with tools to navigate high-stakes conversations, fostering dialogue that leads to positive outcomes.

Online Courses:

1. **Coursera - "Emotional Intelligence" by Case Western Reserve University:** This online course provides a deep dive into emotional intelligence, offering practical tools and strategies for enhancing self-awareness and interpersonal relationships.
2. **LinkedIn Learning - "Building Resilience" by Tatiana Kolovou:** Resilience is a critical soft skill. This course on LinkedIn Learning explores the concept of resilience and provides actionable insights for building mental toughness in the face of challenges.
3. **Udemy - "Practical Psychology for Happiness, Fulfillment and Energy" by Anna Petukova:** creative approach to identify your own motivation and desires. This Udemy course offers practical and effective strategies to alleviate anxiety, providing you with the tools to navigate life's challenges with calm and resilience.
4. **edX - "Leading High-Performing Teams" by University of Queensland:** Collaboration and teamwork are essential soft skills. This course on edX explores strategies for leading high-performing teams, emphasizing the interpersonal dynamics that contribute to team success.

Offline Resources:

1. **Local Workshops and Seminars:** Attend workshops and seminars hosted by local professional organizations, universities, or industry associations. These events provide opportunities for networking and skill-building in a face-to-face setting.

2. **Professional Networking Groups:** Joining local or industry-specific networking groups can expose professionals to diverse perspectives and provide a platform for practicing and refining soft skills through interactions with peers.

3. **Executive Coaching:** Engage in one-on-one executive coaching sessions to receive personalized guidance on soft skill development. Coaches can provide valuable feedback and create tailored plans for improvement.

Applying integration of the resources to a personal development plan can make an important contribution towards continuous soft skill improvement. From integrating knowledge from books, attending online learning resources to actual classes offline – professionals are able to forge a well-orders skill set oriented towards the swiftly developing contemporary setting.

Chapter 7. Networking and Mentorship

In terms of soft skill development, networking and mentorship are different but dynamic aspects that contribute to professional growth. Within this interconnected paradigm, such practices serve as catalysts for expanding knowledge, building meaningful relationships and developing a capacity that goes far behind just technical expertise.

Networking goes beyond the social interaction during events; it is an intentional and persistent endeavor to nurture relationships that can help individuals advance their careers. In social skills, networking is a laboratory for developing the interpersonal communication and relationship-building skills.

One of the main advantages of networking is access to diverse thought patterns. Collaborating with professionals from different sectors, careers and functions also creates a complex mosaic of experiences. These encounters force people to modify their communication strategies, improve active listening skills and empathize with others' points of view.

In addition, networking improves negotiation and teamwork abilities. Navigating professional relationships is an art that entails compromise, fair settlement of conflicts and utilization of collective strengths. Networking helps professionals perfect their skills of persuasion, convincing others to cooperate or work with them in the interests of both parties.

The digital era has made online networking tools an essential element of professional's relationships. Virtual networks, such as LinkedIn or Xing provide an environment to communicate with other peer professionals in the industry, be part of discussions and highlight one's knowledge. Navigating these cyberspaces calls for careful communication and, therefore, demands clarity in expressing one's ideas through a form that can be readily understood by individuals of various backgrounds.

Successful networking also depends on being able to express one's personal brand. In creating such powerful stories about their past and future, soft skills as self-confidence storytelling comes to the surface. Building an effective personal brand does not only make it easy to network but also guarantees a better career, advancements and opportunities.

Mentorship is a reciprocal activity that involves more knowledgeable individuals supporting those with less experience, helping them develop skills. As a dynamic factor in soft skills, mentorship is aimed at developing leadership qualities, emotional intelligence and resilience.

One of the most important benefits that mentorship provides is transferring tacit knowledge. The soft skills, much guided by the experiential learning play a great role in borrowing from veteran mentors' knowledge and inspires. Mentees experience a realistic situation, and they find out how to act in the situations of difficulties, decisions making as well as interpersonal relations.

It also offers a formal channel through which one can expect to receive useful criticism. Feedback is an essential tool for improving soft skills because they are subtle and subjective. Mentors provide personalized advice that allows mentees to pinpoint what needs improvement and give specific steps towards development.

The emotional aspect of mentorship is just as important for the development of soft skills. It can be emotionally difficult to navigate through complex professional terrain, and having a mentor as someone with whom you may sound off provides comfort in that it offers reinforcement and perspective. Mentors often talk about their own experience of overcoming obstacles, building resilience and providing mentees with required emotional intelligence to face the same ones.

The mentor gets to practice their leadership and coaching skills. Helping others implies learning one's own soft skills which makes a mentor ponder over their history and polish interpersonal abilities as well communication capacities.

Synergy of the networking and mentorship increases its effect on soft skill development. The process of networking is essentially the entry point to locate mentors, and through them one's professional network grows. This is a networked system that enables learning and development throughout.

Both offline and online networking events can be a rich place for finding potential mentors. The ability to have a discussion, inquire for advice or reply with interested comments on someone's experience can develop over time into mentorship. On the other hand, mentors can connect mentees to their networks allowing new access for contacts and information.

The idea of reciprocity in mentoring supports the philosophy behind proper networking. As mentees mature in their advancements, they can develop into mentors themselves propagating the flow of knowledge shared among professionals. This spiraling process provides a self-sustaining basis for developing soft skills where wisdom acquired from mentors is continually passed through ongoing networking interactions.

Networking and mentorship have a collaborative element that defines the teamwork framework, which is itself an important soft skill in any setting. People with developed network and mentoring skills demonstrate high competence in the area of relationship building, which is creating an environment for teamwork within their organization.

As professionals actively participate in network development, they use the occasions to perfect communication and bargaining skills as well as relationship management. Concurrently, mentoring provides a structured mechanism for both guidance and feedback as well supportive emotional resources that encourage the development of leadership qualities and resilience. The interdependence between networking and mentorship results in a symbiotic relationship that promotes ongoing learning. These practices, through a reciprocal exchange of knowledge and experiences that leads to the development of competence in handling professional terrain effectively.

As such, soft skill acquisition through networking and mentorship is a process rather than an end. Accordingly, professionals embark on a lifelong journey of learning as they incorporate these practices into the workplace and gain valuable connections and mentors who positively influence their professional lives.

If only personal and career advancement is considered vital in the professional world, strategic networking with built support system as well mentorship opportunities should also be indispensable. These intertwined processes are even more than traditional career transitions – they contribute to solid and resilient professional momentum.

While networking is considered to be a professional necessity, the actual secret of it lies in building an interpersonal environment that helps its members overcome common issues. Here are key strategies for building a supportive professional network:

Building a genuine relationship with people is the basis of good networking. Authenticity cultivates trust and promotes true connection. Professionals should not only focus on their professional interests, but also pay more attention to the person behind the job title in order to build long-term relationships.

The strengths of the network lie in its diversity people from different backgrounds, industries and roles. The implications of broadening one's network, not only new ideas are gained but also opportunities for cooperation and mentorship. The expansion of the network through interaction with professionals from other fields enriches it.

In the age of digital technology, an online footprint is a valuable networking instrument. Utilizing platforms such as LinkedIn facilitates professionals to interact with people worldwide, share thoughts and engage in discussions within their fields. Keeping a professional and up-to date digital identity increases visibility, which assists in the online networking.

Physical and online networking events help people to meet individuals with similar interests. A friendly atmosphere allows attendees to exchange their stories, talk about current industry trends and develop relationships. Taking part in such events – local meetups or worldwide conferences helps to build networks.

While mentorship involves the transfer of knowledge, it is significantly more than that; there are elements such as guidance, advice and counselling interaction. Here are strategies for seeking mentorship opportunities.

When looking for a mentor, it is vital to define both personal and professional objectives. Knowing what one intends to benefit from the relationship is a way of identifying mentors whose life experiences match their intentions. With set expectations, a mentorship relationship has direction and purpose.

In coming up with potential mentors, it involves identifying people whose journey, knowledge and that is buying into the value system among those being mentored. This investigation can be performed through such professional networks, industry events or online sites. Selecting mentors who have overcome similar predicaments or accomplished significant success considerably enhances the quality of a mentorship program.

Meaningful dialogues form the basis of becoming a mentor. Sharing interests, asking for advice on certain problems or genuine praise of the mentor's work can be a basis for developing such connection. Essential roles are played by authenticity and sincerity in rapport building.

An effective mentorship relationship involves willingness to take advice and receive critical feedback. Mentees need to be open-minded and ready for change in order to benefit from the revelations that their mentors have provided them with. First of all, being open to others' advice is key to a healthy mentor-mentee relationship. Mentorship is not a one-off affair but instead an ongoing relationship that develops over time. The mentees should strive to establish lasting relationship with their mentors. Regular follow-ups, updates on achievements and positive expressions help to consolidate the mentorship relation.

The tactics for establishing a strong professional network and finding mentorship possibilities are threads that weave an intricate tapestry of career development. The developed professional network includes authentic connection, diversification, reciprocal engagement, digital presence and active participations in networking events.

Since we finish the journey of Principle 7, 'Sharpen the Soft Skill Saw', it has been an enlightening expedition while highlighting how pivotal soft skills are within tech industry's hostile climate. While considering the importance of sharpening these capacities continuously, it becomes clear that they are not just a complement to technological competence but an essential basis for professional success and well-roundedness.

Soft skills, also known as human or interpersonal skills are gaining more importance in the world of technology. As technology progresses, so does the demand for people who are efficient in their communication and collaborative abilities as a way to adapt. The essence of the technology industry mandates a workforce that is able to navigate through complicated social relations, add value in group activities and display emotional intelligence.

In such a dynamic environment where innovation and change are the hallmarks, adaptability - this ability to communicate effectively becomes as important as technical knowledge. This principle touched different aspects of soft skills, from communication and collaboration to problem-solving and adaptability. It emphasized empathy, active listening and understanding the needs of stakeholders as part of a complete skill set.

The principle emphasized the importance of continuous improvement and encouraged professionals to consider soft skills as a continuously evolving part of their skill set. It became evident that being up to date on the industry trends, discovering gaps in one's personal skill set, and developing individual development plans were important for keeping constant growth. The idea recognized that the learning journey is not fixed and has no end point but a process of improvement.

It was also discussed how agile methodologies and soft skills can work together to enhance innovativeness, drive success in a project setting. The principle also recognized that such a collaborative and communicable environment is the enriching soil on which agile principles grow. Applications of cases showed how teams synergizing agile and soft skills in order to positively impact the project results.

When technology changes, soft skills remain the same asset throughout time. It is to glue different teams, the guiding principle of effective communication and catalyst for problem-solving innovation. In the unstable world of technological development, where challenges are as prevalent as opportunities that professionals armed with soft skills is well prepared to meet all possible difficulties and manage it effectively.

After concluding the discussion on Principle 7, we imagine a future where tech professionals integrate agile methodologies with their continually honed soft skills. This fusion results in a workforce that not only adapts to technological innovations but also flourishes when cooperation, sympathy and flexibility are put into action. Principle 7 is a thread that binds individual skill sets across the grand tapestry of professional growth accounting for collective achievement and innovation. The traveling to sharpen the soft skill saw is an ongoing one and as professionals undertake this continuous improvement, they not only better their lot but contribute towards strengthening to our resilience of tech Ecosystem.

Conclusion. 7 habits of highly effective tech people

At the end of our study, we continue in a critical reflective journey that captures key principles underlying success. As we concentrate the knowledge of each paradigm, we bring to light a woven cloth blending hard skills and the essential fabric of soft skills that tells us about any individual's total career development in terms by an account balance.

The foundational principles we discussed throughout this book reinforce the belief that technical knowledge alone does not serve as a prerequisite for success in the tech industry. On the contrary, it is actually a complementary interaction between technical skill and soft skills that drives people or teams towards high performance. Whereas soft skills are generally pushed to the outskirts, they appear as drivers that contribute towards successful communication, cooperation and continuous development.

The trip started with the needs of being proactive in professional development showing that a growth mindset, continuous learning and deliberate career development need to be pursued. The professionals were to move with deliberation through the career path in order that it approaches acquiring skills and taking resort for overcoming challenges as rungs.

The chapter "Begin with the End in Mind" helped people map an ambitious path for their technical leader role. The principle emphasized the need for long-term goal setting, a culture of empowerment and how leaders negotiate common leadership obstacles. Using examples from the real world, leaders could make sure that they begin clearly then their tribes follow a common path of success.

Adaptability became the guiding light and led tech professionals through how to master in a quick manner. By studying the connection between adaptability and time management, we presented solutions for a better task prioritization process and an increase in agility. This adaptive journey entailed overcoming resistance to change as well as developing leadership skills under any conditions.

This collaborative spirit infused around the discourse on cross-functional cooperation, highlighting a win-win mentality. Collaboration challenges were discovered, and solutions to them discussed. The principle demonstrated the power of communication, negotiation and compromise as well the creation of a culture that rewards team work.

Problem-solving that worked became a pillar, tightly linked with the understanding of another's suffering. At the forefront of problem solving, active listening; stakeholder needs understanding and communication skills honing. The real-life cases highlighted how understanding and user-oriented processes resulted in positive results.

The relationship between agile methodologies and soft skills became the centerpiece, reflecting how cooperation, communication, and flexibility act as trigger agents for success in an agile environment. The concept discussed the role of synergy, showing case studies that involved synthesis agile and soft skills to achieve perfect results.

The final principle supported ongoing soft skill development, acknowledging them as mutable components of professional advancement. Ongoing improvement strategies, networking ideas, mentor frameworks and customized development plans. The principle culminated in a hands-on soft skill development workshop, facilitating active participation during the journey of refinement.

As we knit these principles to each other, the same string appears - the zeal towards constant progression. The technology sector, which is distinguished by constant innovation and evolution, requires professionals not only to learn the ins and outs of technological processes but also develop social skills needed for customization in the dynamic environment.

On this grand canvas of developing tech with soft skills, we observe a transformation - a move away from the concept of an isolated individualistic and technically driven professional towards all-roundedness. Success is transformed into a group accomplishment, characterized by partnerships, empathy, and constant development as the basis of an environment that flourishes.

In the end, as we move back from this transformative experience, it is time to act. The appeal to professionals in the tech sector is that they should consider a balanced approach towards careers personal mastery, which encompasses both hardware and software skills visionary leadership adaptability collaborative spirit persistence.

This becomes not just an option but a necessity, in the dynamic world of technology where change is constancy. This book acts as a manual that calls for people to join in the exploration of self-revelation, development and complementary work ethics because on end both technical knowledge need not count well with soft skills if growth is supposed be achieved.

Holistic Growth

Understanding holistic growth through the lens of a career path in tech requires an appreciation for how technical and soft skills are intrinsically tied together. It is an understanding that transcends the traditional focus on technical competence, recognizing that a successful career requires balancing and integration of different skills.

Let us consider a practitioner working in the tech industry, which is ever changing. While they climb the ladder of technical skill, from proficiency in programming languages to grasping complex system structures and even venturing into advanced data analytics, soft skills become a subtle but essential thread running through their travels.

Effective communication is the bridge that links highly technical ideas to articulated concepts. When collaboration becomes a driver, it enables the effective implementation of projects that require teamwork. Adaptability enables smooth passage through all the changing demands of a project. Problem solving becomes a collective practice through incorporation of different viewpoints to generate creative solutions.

In the current professional world, companies tend to look for potential employees who can offer not only high-tech knowledge but a comprehensive skill set as well. This skill set includes communication, teamwork, adaptation and emotional intelligence to create an environment for soft skills. In this matrix of skills, professionals are more prepared due to the interdisciplinary nature of their profession.

At the heart of this connectivity is emotional intelligence which forms a pillar in soft skills. The emotional intelligence allows people to understand and control their emotions in addition to the complicated world of others' feelings. It serves as the catalyst that promotes healthy work relationships, good leadership and maneuvering complex interpersonal situations.

Soft skills play an even greater role in the team where cross-functional collaboration is a common template. The advent of a collaborative culture is the result of professionals who are versatile to both technical and soft skills. This environment, on the other hand, serves as a fertile ground for innovation where different viewpoints come together to address complex issues.

Tech leadership requires more than technical skills. An important element of good leadership is visionary stewardship, empathy and flexibility to withstand challenges. An understanding leader who knows the interdependence between technical and soft skills will also encourage teams, create a healthy atmosphere, change behaviors depending on situations.

The concept of holistic development also encompasses notions such as lifelong learning and adaptivity. A growth mindset combined with a focus on lifelong learning is thus highly advantageous in today's dynamic tech environment because it allows professionals to stay ahead of the curve. In this process, soft skills play a crucial part as they make learning effective and enable people to work in teams comprised of various groups making them adaptive acquiring new knowledge.

When we consider the concept of holistic growth, it is possible to see through a lens that reveals an image of systematic success. As a result, the link between hard and soft skills is not seen in terms of an opposition but rather as something harmonious to contribute to enriching professional life. This principle encourages specialists to take a holistic view of their professional arsenal, recognizing that real progress in the tech sphere comes from technical savoir-faire and soft skills woven together. Individuals create a story of continued success, while dealing with the changing nature and demands of technology innovation.

Commitment to Continuous Improvement

Continuous improvement stands as an anchor at the cutting edge of tech industry where it is constantly changing. It is a promise to undertake endless journey of learning, refining and improving one's skills. This dedication, especially as far as soft skills are concerned goes beyond the concept of a fixed skill set and embraces the perpetuality in terms of personal or professional development.

As a driving force, continuous improvement leads such people to reconsider their path in life not only professionally but also privately. It induces a reflective analysis of previous events, celebrating achievements while embracing lessons drawn from the pain. With this process of reflection, a person earns the positive aspects due to strengths in his or her knowledge and gaps for one prompting action with technical-based skills

In terms of soft skills, continuous improvement entails a perpetual analysis on communication efficiency, group dynamics cooperation amid various setting and the subtle mastery associated with trouble-shooting. It highlights the fact that success in these domains is not a destination but an endless journey. This commitment is not to earn skills but perfect and magnify them over time.

The fundamental pillar of this undertaking is the understanding that soft skills, just as technical skills are malleable. These skills operate in a constantly changing context due to the workplace environment, societal dynamics and technological advancements. As a result, people who are dedicated to continuous improvement pay attention to the rhythm of these changes and get ready for adjustment and soft skills toolkit enhancement in accordance with those.

The continuous improvement journey does not involve one person. It does particularly well in an environment that is supportive and cooperative. An environment in which open discussions and knowledge sharing among peers are encouraged ensure everyone is invested in the progress of their counterparts. This shared mindset intensifies the effects of continuous improvement, as observations and know-how from different points of view fill a common bank of knowledge.

In addition, the ongoing development policy practically complies with agile methodologies since collaboration and adaptability are integral parts of these approaches. People engaging in continuous improvement inherently identify with agile practices and its recursive nature, seeing reflection, adaptation as well as advancement manifested in their propensity.

Some pragmatic measures that readers ready to constantly improve themselves should consider are routine self-assessments, peer and mentor critiques as well as involvement in professional development initiatives. These methods make it possible to act on the principle of proactive growth; thus, every success or failure becomes a platform for development.

This internalized commitment to continuous improvement acts as a catalyst in one's career. It conceptualizes the career path as an endless perfection pursuit, where technical and soft skill mastery becomes a constant struggle. This promise does not confine itself in time or is thought to be flattening; instead, it represents a determination for sailing through rough seas of technology without tiring and with much vigor.

Adaptability in a Dynamic Industry

This dynamic pattern of the tech industry is agility, which impacts not only individual lifestyles but also organizations. Even though the rate of technological progress, accompanied by changes in market needs indicates that professionals should have adaptiveness as chief competency.

The core of adaptability is the ability to manage change, so that endurance and flexibility are ensured. This is a realization that the only thing stable in tech innovation is change. As technologies develop, paradigms are shifted and what was new yesterday might be obsolete tomorrow. In this kind of environment, professionals who assert adaptiveness not only survive; they thrive.

Adaptability is not a passive response about change, but an idea of it. In fact, it is a process of life-long education as the permanent change through unlearning and relearning. For this reason, professionals are able to challenge themselves and see new challenges as opportunities for development rather than hardships they cannot overcome. They use change to promote innovation and evolution. An agile professional is not only proficient at learning various programming languages but also efficient in building respectful cultures and sharing knowledge among different teams.

Further, adaptability becomes more critical when one considers the interdependence of global tech realm. Professionals now work as part of globally distributed teams, cooperating on different time zones and cultural landscapes. Adaptability, therefore becomes the cement that glues together teams so diverse and yet each individual is able to integrate his or her wide range of views into this environment.

For organizations, the building of an adaptable culture is a strategic necessity. Such an approach entails the development of a necessary environment that allows employees to experiment, innovate and embrace change. And leaders are instrumental in influencing this culture by promoting a learning mindset, presenting opportunities for growth and development, imbuing adaptability as an essential competency.

With the dynamics of the tech industry changing so fast, adaptability becomes a pivot towards success. It is not a perishable skill but an enduring mindset that enables professionals to deal with uncertainty, embrace change and drive innovation. In a world dominated by uncertainty, the ability to adjust is not only relevant in terms of career protection but also adds resilience and vigor for the entire tech landscape.

To the individuals who are starting out, as well as those with more experience in this undertaking I am fully confident that you will be able to use and apply tools of soft skills for unprecedented levels of success in technology. As you walk through the terrain of adaptability, teamwork, management and problem solving, remember that you have within your grasp all it takes to navigate obstacles and make opportunities work for us.

Comforting soft skills is not an option; it's a strategic move that will make you stand out in the tech industry. You are not just passive observers of change; you create it. Your dedication to ongoing improvement and comprehensive development is not just about your careers alone but will also help elevate tech ecosystem as a whole.

When venturing into developing success via soft skills, your path should be viewed as an eternal expedition rather than a destination. The ideas discussed in this exploration do not stay the same; they change, just as your industry changes. Your dedication to bootstrap learning, constant progress and the harmonization of soft skills with tech expertise places you on an innovative path in the field.

I urge you not to consider challenges as impossibilities, rather they are occasions for improving adaptability, leadership and problem-solving abilities. There is a lesson to be learned in every failure and an avenue for advancing yourself after every victory. You have a non-linear journey, and success is not standardized. It is a journey tailored specifically for you, in which every turn and twist contributes to your development.

Therefore, let this be a call to action. Use these principles as a guide in your daily activities. Try to network with people, be inspirational and let others do the work. Recognize that every situation is an opportunity to perfect your communication and active listening abilities. Tackle problems not like unscalable mountains but as unsolved puzzles that can be solved through creative thinking.

In such a world of technology marked by swift improvements and continuous disruptions, your dedication to soft skills is what keeps you ahead. It is the magic component that turns a competent professional into an irreplaceable asset. In investing into your soft skills, you are thereby in favor of adaptability and team spirit along with leadership development as well problem-solving being the paramount pillars onto which success leans on this industry.

Be aware that success is not solely yours. It is a collective effort in that your development contributes to the overall progress of technology as a whole. Your success does not stop at personal accomplishments; it reverberates in the partnerships you inspire, your role model leadership and how well you address problems.

Finally, I wish you not only success but satisfaction in your technical pursuits. May your flexibility serve as your compass, collaboration be an indicator of strength, leadership provide the directing light; may problem-solving skills become a superpower help. And here's to the future filled with innovation, development and significant achievements that will be part of technology fabric. May you traverse it with strength, guide others in the right direction and be an example to those around. Forward to a future where your tech and soft skills merge for unprecedented success.